Between Worlds

Between Worlds
A collection of essays

S. Nadja Zajdman

Bridge House

© Copyright 2024
S. Nadja Zajdman
The right of S. Nadja Zajdman to be identified as author of this work has been asserted by her in accordance with the Copyright, Designs and Patents Act 1988

All rights reserved

No parts of this publication may be reproduced, stored in a retrieval system, or transmitted in any form or by any means, electronic, mechanical, photocopying, recording or otherwise without prior permission of the copyright owner.

British Library Cataloguing in Publication Data
A Record of this Publication is available from the British Library

ISBN 978-1-914199-84-4

This edition published 2024 by Bridge House Publishing
Manchester, England

For my parents. Until we meet again.

CONTENTS

INTRODUCTION 9
BETWEEN WORLDS 10
AN UNRECORDED PERFORMANCE 20
A PORTRAIT IN TIME 23
THE MAN IN THE RAINCOAT 27
OPEN HEARTED 32
WHAT'S IN A NAME 40
DON'T ASK 42
"NANA" 44
"DADDY KAYE" 46
UPSETTING SANTA 50
TUESDAY'S CHILD 53
NOT MARY POPPINS 55
THE SHOW MUST GO ON 58
SOMEONE TO WATCH OVER ME 61
THE BEST PLAY HE NEVER SAW 64
AN ANGEL AT OUR TABLE 68
UNTIL WE MEET AGAIN 72
HEY MA, LOOK AT ME 77
MIKEY'S VISION 81
INSULT AND INJURY 85
SETTING THE TEMPLATE 91

COMMUNIST HOT DOGS, IN PURSUIT OF PETULA, AND A KISS FROM MARLENE DIETRICH 93

MY SECRET ADMIRER 97

OUR P.E.T. 99

BLOOMING WHERE WE'RE PLANTED, AND A TASTE OF HONEY 103

REMOVING SOCIAL MASKS 110

THE WONDERFUL WORLD OF TRAVEL 113

LET THE GOOD TIMES ROLL 122

THE SOUNDTRACK OF OUR LIVES 124

ERIC'S SECRET 127

INTENSIVE CARE 144

FINDING MY FEET 159

MOUNTAIN GUIDE 162

EUREKA SPRINGS REVISITED 166

GOING HOLLYWOOD 173

BENE MERITO: THE STORY OF EWA JANINA WOCJICKA 194

HOW MY MUM CAME TO FORGIVE OMAR SHARIF 212

THE END OF THE BEGINNING 214

OUTTAKE 219

BETWEEN WORLDS 225

INTRODUCTION

This volume contains a collection of essays published over the last twenty years. Inescapably, most are dominated by the spirit of my spectacular mother. Since the untimely death of my father, by default Mum and I became the longest, the most intimate and intense relationship of each other's lives.

My irrepressible dad springs up in this volume, as does my irresistible brother. There are portraits of loved ones long gone. Writing about them was my way of keeping them close.

There is a nod to the period of the pandemic, though I did not write about the pandemic so much as write my way through it. For me, the pandemic years were a highly creative time.

The piece *Bene Merito* is an exception. It is the story of a woman Mum considered her surrogate mother. When she was terminally ill, Mum asked me to write this story. It was a daunting task, but I set myself to it in order to honour what amounted to my mother's last wish, as well as to honour the memory of a wartime heroine without whom Mum would not have survived, and those left behind would never have existed.

The rest of these essays reflect my eclectic tastes and enthusiasms. Hopefully, they will appeal to the reader, too.

S. Nadja Zajdman Montreal, Canada, June 2024

BETWEEN WORLDS

I first became aware of him during a war crimes trial. He was capital M masculine: dark, brooding, and intense. He defended the indefensible. He seemed to have sprung from the wrong side of history, and he had me from the instant the camera zoomed in on his chiselled features, as if compelled to do so by his command. I couldn't keep my eyes off him. I would keep an eye on him and the other eye out for him to the end of his life, and beyond.

Born into the sound of music, raised in Heidi-Land and acclaimed in Hollywood, Maximilian Schell returned to the clamour and ferment of Western Europe's mid-twentieth century cultural life to reinvent himself as a stage and film director and director of operas, and as a pianist professional enough to perform with Leonard Bernstein. All the while he continued waging the last necessary war over and over again in film, both in the character of Nazis, as well as in the characters of their Jewish victims, as if he felt guilty for having spent the period of the actual war in neutral Switzerland – or as if he couldn't make up his mind.

Ultimately Schell lived with, and in the last months of his life he married a decades-younger opera singer who looked like Heidi. Schell had returned to his roots, to his mother's family estate in the Austrian Alps, and there he would die and be buried, like Heidi's grandfather, in the pastoral splendour of The Alm.

The image and influence of Maximilian Schell ran current and counterpoint to my fifteen-minute career as an actress, along with my inheritance of the Holocaust, which I received through my mother. Because of this heritage and out of deference to my mother's sensibilities I kept hidden my affinity for *Mittel Europa*, which may have been an Ernst Lubitsch fantasy even while it existed. Yet my maternal grandfather studied in Zurich during the First World War and my maternal grandmother studied opera in Vienna, so why should I not feel the pull of an alternate world I might've been born into, if that world hadn't rejected my grandparents? Why did I consider such an attraction aberrant?

I had an extended and intricate – albeit one-sided – relationship with Maximilian Schell. I followed his first directorial efforts in little cinema venues, where they would run for a week. My mother was amused by my fascination with "that aging German", yet indulgent. She even accompanied me to the screenings, letting her guard down, and confessing, "Kid, ya got good taste."

Still, my mother withheld full approval. In the years before we both matured, in my mother's mind, any German of her generation was suspect until proven innocent. Paradoxically Schell's older sister Maria, a shooting star of the 1950s, enchanted Mum. Though her younger brother's career would soon leave Maria's in the dust, the lovely Teutonic maiden who smiled winsomely through tears was firmly entrenched in my mother's melancholy heart.

The other part Schell was born to play was the schizophrenic, or self-destructive character of a Jewish Holocaust survivor who takes on the identity of a Nazi war criminal so that Israeli hunters will find him, try him, and supposedly execute him – or was the character really the said Nazi hiding in the open as a Jewish Holocaust survivor? Originally a stage play, *The Man in the Glass Booth*, patterned on Eichmann and his trial, was so controversial that in Montreal, when a production was scheduled at The Saidye Bronfman Center Theatre (known today as The Segal Center Theatre), thugs from the Jewish Defence League planted portions of the script, out of context, in the mailboxes of Jewish homes, and threatened to bomb the theatre if it went forward with its plans. The theatre's artistic director, a French Jew born to Polish parents and, like my mother, a survivor of wartime Warsaw, had dropped his last name and used the French version of his middle name. Thus, in the local theatre milieu, he was known by the stage name of Marion André. This time under threat of physical violence from Jews, Marion André resigned in disgust and left for the brighter lights and keener minds of Toronto.

Several years later the American Film Theatre Institute, as part of its mandate to film and preserve great plays with great actors, produced a filmed version of *The Man in the Glass Booth*. Who to cast in the lead role was a no-brainer. Everything Schell had done and stood for led to this moment and this part. In movie palaces across North America, audiences flocked to see the mind-bending *Man in the Glass Booth*.

In Montreal, at the now-defunct Van Horne Theatre, the film was presented as a special event. As in live theatre, printed programs were prepared. The audience for this one-night-only screening consisted of the same people who, several years earlier, were provoked into raising a stink putrid enough to shut down a theatrical production and drive its director out of the province. There seemed to be collective amnesia surrounding the hysteria of several years past.

On this breezy spring evening Our Crowd came out to socialize, to hail the play, to laud the performance of the international star Schell, and to ask themselves, and each other, "Is he Jewish?" Some were questioning the identity of the character Schell played. Some were questioning Schell's credentials.

In those days, long before the advent of the Internet, there was no way of prying into the private life of a public person unless he was popular enough to be of interest to movie magazines, or notorious enough to be of interest to the tabloids. In North America, Schell was neither, so there was a blackout on information that might reveal the private man. In the theatre-style program that was provided for the filmed event, I picked up the first clues to Schell's origins, and his sympathies. "Born in Vienna, 1930... in 1938 he moved to Switzerland..." Since Schell was eight years old at the time of this "move," one assumed his parents moved with him.

"See Ma!" I exulted, pointing to the biography in the program. "He isn't German, he's SWISS German!" My sceptical mother perused the program. The nuances embedded in the truncated biography were even more obvious to her than they were to me.

"Alright." My mother allowed herself a smile. "He's *kosher*."

What a relief. I plopped in my seat. Now that Mama had accepted him, the path was clear. Maximilian could marry me when I grew up – or when I came of age, at least.

When I was thirty, I dreamt a riotous dream. I was in a brilliantly lit ballroom. I was elegantly gowned. I was standing next to an equally elegant, tuxedoed Maximilian Schell but I was the center of attention, because I was his bride-to-be.

The greats of the German-speaking film and theatre world were in attendance, both the living and the dead, along with a couple of outsiders. There was a monocled Fritz Lang, who puffed smoke from a gold-tipped cigarette inserted in a long-stemmed holder, into the pixie-like visage of a sour-looking Peter Lorre. There was a shimmering Marlene Dietrich, who had no eyebrows, but was sporting a top hat, white tie and tails. There was a scruffy Bertholt Brecht, who had refused to don a tie, but was welcomed anyway. After a cursory greeting, Brecht makes a beeline for the heavily laden buffet, and stuffs bread rolls into his over-sized pockets. Dietrich sidles up to Hedy Lamarr, while Anton Walbrook drools discreetly over my Max whom, I realize with a start, I will have to, forever after, call Max, because Maximilian takes too long to say.

At the far end of the ballroom, on a love seat, lounges a bearded Sigmund Freud. The doctor of the subconscious smiles knowingly at Schell while, in an opposite corner of the vast reception hall, Freud's protégé and rival Carl Jung smiles knowingly at me.

Above it all, an ebullient Ernst Lubitsch swings on a blazing crystal chandelier. He has taken it upon himself to stage this phantasmagoria. All the while I wonder; if we are in the German-speaking world, why is everyone addressing me, and each other, in English?

"*Liebschen,*" explains my Max. "We're in your dream. You have to be able to understand it."

Surreptitiously, like a conscience, through a hidden entrance Theodore Bikel sneaks into the hall. He is wearing a white shirt open at the collar, casual slacks, and sandals. He has a guitar strapped to his back. The teddy-bear-like Bikel shifts his guitar to the front of his burly torso and, standing next to a set of French windows, presses his back against the wall. Positioning his guitar, he strums and hums, "I kiss your hand, Madam, wishing it were more..." Bikel lifts his guitar pick, glares at me, and abruptly stops. "Don't do it." Bikel's glance shoots darts at me. "*Maidele,* please don't do it."

From his perch atop the chandelier, Lubitsch spies Bikel and tries to shoo him out of the picture and out of my dream. At that moment Conrad Veidt and his last and Jewish spouse stroll arm-in-arm into my vision and viewpoint.

"It can work, *liebschen*," Veidt encourages me, and dismisses Bikel. "Look at us." He beams beatifically at his beloved Lily. "It can work."

I say nothing, but think to myself, "Your marriage worked because you gave the finger to Goebbels and fled to England in '33. Then you gave away your life savings to support the British war effort, and crossed the ocean to Hollywood only to end up playing Nazis. Your marriage worked because you lived Here, and not There." Except that I am now disoriented, and can no longer distinguish between Here and There. In the literal world, I am alone and asleep in my bed in Montreal. In my dream, I am in a ballroom in Munich because, in the 1980s, Munich has become the center of the German-speaking film world. Max must be here for his work.

I avert my eyes from Veidt and raise them towards Max.

"We won't be living here all the time. We can live some of the time in Switzerland. You promised." Though I am over the moon to have bagged Max, I feel guilty about the prospect of living on the continent that hounded my mother out of it.

I receive no clear answer from my dream-state *inamorata*. Instead, I wake up.

A few weeks after experiencing this dream, my mother called, gleefully needling me.

"I've got news for you!" Mum trumpeted, and she didn't break it gently. "I read in the newspaper that Maximilian Schell just got married to a Russian actress twenty-five years younger than he is! Too bad, sweetheart! Hee hee!" This marriage was the actress' second marriage. Surprisingly, or maybe not, at the age of fifty-five, it was Schell's first.

"Oh leave me alone!" I moaned into the receiver. I was stung by the loss of my fantasy. I was also flabbergasted at learning that, on the other side of the world, an exact contemporary had realized my dream.

It would not be until fourteen months after Schell's sudden death that I stumbled onto news of it. I was at the bottom of a well of bereavement. I had recently lost my mother.

Certainly I didn't grieve for Maximilian the way I grieved for my mother, but the news of his death was the first piece of news to pierce the placenta of anguish that separated me from the living world. If my mother had outlived him, we would've commiserated over his passing. If Mum had heard about it first then, this piece of news, she would've broken to me gently.

On my own, almost obsessively, I entered into the virtual world of the Internet. I discovered the details of Schell's back-story, and was able to follow the events that unfolded in the aftermath of his death. His funeral appeared to be a state funeral. His Russian ex-wife did not attend, though Schell's stepson, the offspring of her first marriage, delivered the eulogy.

The sombre funeral procession through a pristine Alpine village might've been staged by Schell. It was the dead of winter. The fresh snow was piled high. The bleakness of the landscape and the mourners' black attire were juxtaposed in stark contrast to a whited-out world.

Then came the aftermath. Astonishingly, a man in his eighties, with a very young wife and an even younger daughter, left no legal testament.

Surfing the net, I weaved in and out of the distant past and recent past, watching Schell, at the height of his power and beauty, receive his one and only Oscar from the hands of a middle-aged Joan Crawford; watching Schell, in old age, in his Alpine retreat, flip sadly through a family album, revisiting his dead parents and his sisters.

I delved into Schell's romantic history, which proved densely populated. His taste in women remained consistent. No matter how old he got, Schell preferred his partners to be around the age of thirty. No matter how old he got, the women Schell preferred responded.

Schell's marriage to the Russian actress did not last, but it produced a daughter who was born when he was close to sixty. His last love was an opera singer who is German, whose birthday is one day away from Hitler's birthday, whose name isn't Heidi, yet I came to think of her that way.

The couple kept an apartment in Vienna, and retreated regularly to the family estate on The Alm. The magical technology of this century allowed me to visit Maximilian on his private alpine meadow. I entered the upscale, well-equipped, and immaculate living area that was referred to, ingenuously, as a "hut". At the far end I could glimpse the kitchen where Schell cooked potato dishes and prepared his favourite repast, which was *wiener schnitzel*, no less, serving dinner to the young woman who drove up the perilous mountain pass to be with him, after a period of stage work in Vienna. Like a good director, Schell left her notes.

Schell had slowed; he had mellowed. He achieved more than most artists can hope to accomplish in a lifetime, and now he mentored the young woman he had drawn in and made part of what was left of his life.

A baby grand piano served as the living room's centrepiece. In clement weather the windows were open so that when "Heidi" played, the sound of music mingled with the sounds of nature. It was the sound of music that brought "Heidi" and the elderly Schell together.

Having inherited, or claimed, the Alpine retreat, after Schell's death "Heidi" still kept its windows open and still played its piano while breezes lifted and carried the sound of music to the nearby family burial plot.

As I continued to research, my fascination with Schell shifted to his young widow. She must have had more than prettiness and youth to hold such a man. I intrude upon her virtual person. "Heidi" had a burgeoning career, when she first met Schell. Now, on her own, she continues to work. Financially, she needs to work. Emotionally, she needs to work even more.

During the course of their unconventional relationship, which most people considered an inappropriate one, it was "Heidi" who bore the brunt of the public's scurrilous curiosity.

"Has being the girlfriend (sic) of the great Maximilian Schell opened doors for you?" A female interviewer snidely inquires.

"It has opened some doors." Heidi admits. "It has also closed others." Ah. I begin to admire this by-no-means dumb blonde.

Schell's widow was widely criticized for auctioning off his art collection. She was pilloried for selling a portrait of Maria Schell. Rightfully so. Hadn't my mother stripped her walls when I first moved into my present apartment in order to live in close proximity to her, installing the portraits of the ancestors onto my walls? I promised I would keep the ancestors safe, and I do. How dare this *rotznase* part with the portrait of the mythic Maria! I grew impatient when I read this. As far as I was concerned, Maria Schell should've been kept in the family.

I lost patience with the dead Maximilian, too. Why didn't you make a will, I berate him, in my mind, as if he could hear me, as if my opinion mattered. You old fool. I hear my mother chastise. Did you think you were going to live forever? You should've known better than to leave a mess!

Periodically I would check in on Heidi to see how she was coping. She told interviewers who monitored her progress, and as time went on, there were less of them, that she was crying less. Heidi began to spend less time in retreat on The Alm.

Within three years of Schell's death, his widow gave birth to a daughter who was sired by a young relative of Schell's. She will always be tied to the Schell family now. She will never be alone again.

My mother and Maximilian Schell were born two years apart and died two months apart. In the decade since they've been gone, I've come to realize that the Aryan actor with the *weltzschmerz* and the war orphan who transcended her war were flip sides of the same coin that came together in me.

―――――――――

WRITTEN 2014, REVISED 2024

AN UNRECORDED PERFORMANCE

As a child in the late 1960s, the first live professional performance I was taken to was a concert with Theodore Bikel. The concert was my birthday present from my mother. Other children got parties; I was exposed to great performances. The evening with Bikel set the template for birthdays to come. My mother was enthralled by Bikel's concert. On that black and damp night in early winter, I didn't think much of the dark-haired teddy bear of a man who sat alone on the stage telling stories, strumming a guitar and singing in half-a-dozen different languages. After all, my father could do these things too, except that he didn't play a guitar. On a warm evening in July of 2012 I was finally able to reciprocate the gift my mother gave me so long ago. I took my now elderly mother to the Segal Center in Montreal to see Bikel in a one-man show he had co-created with his wife, entitled *Sholom Aleichem, Laughter Through Tears.* I had secured a seat for my mother close to the stage while I sat in the last row of the theatre, watching over her.

At the age of eighty-eight, Bikel's singing voice has lost its power though, as an actor, he is as powerful as ever. There were moments when Bikel's singing voice seemed in danger of breaking, as his heart must be breaking. Tamara Brooks, Bikel's long-time companion and wife of the past four years, died of a heart attack in late May, at the age of seventy. She was a musical conductor for thirty-five years until she met and began working with Bikel. She was supposed to have accompanied him at the piano. That this legend honoured his commitment to the theatre and opened the show without her added poignancy to an already poignant performance resonating with ghosts. When Bikel came on stage and announced, "I don't pretend to be characters; I become them," his statement was backed up by my recollection of the film characters into whom this actor had submerged his personality. Then Bikel kept his promise and became the author of the character he is most associated with; Tevye the Milkman. In a ninety-minute solo performance that would've taxed an actor a fraction of his age, Bikel populated the stage with the vanished phantoms of Aleichem's literary landscape, as though they were flowing directly from the author's pen. The images of Bikel's film characters lurked in the shadows, bearing silent witness to a life highlighted by professional triumph, as well as seared by recent personal tragedy.

The average age of the audience that attended this performance was eighty, and their faces were etched with lines testifying to their own triumphs and pain. From my vantage point in the last row I looked out over a sea of snowy-haired heads bobbing like whitecaps on breaking waves. I felt one with them.

Bikel emerged from behind his characters and stepped forward. Behind him was a backdrop of an enlarged photograph of the actor as a young man, consulting over a script with the producer of Fiddler on the Roof, a photograph of Sholom Aleicheim superimposed in the lower right corner of the screen, and another photograph superimposed in the upper left corner; that of Bikel as Tevye. Spectators gripping canes, spectators who had shuffled into the theatre on walkers struggled to their feet in a collective roar of applause and appreciation. If Bikel could stand and perform for them, then they could stand in homage. Bikel brought forward the musicians who had accompanied him. A young male pianist had replaced Bikel's wife. The actor simultaneously acknowledged and dismissed the audience. Brusquely he bowed and then turned away, a theatrical giant suddenly shrinking into a lonely old widower as he trudged off the stage and entered the darkness of the wings, the love of his life no longer waiting there to accompany him home.

I descended the stairs to join my mother, who sat stiffly in her seat, waiting for me like a child waits to be collected by a parent. My octogenarian, widowed mother is chronically ill now, and had been having a particularly difficult day. She had dragged herself out of bed and dressed elegantly in order to honour the ticket I had arranged for her. Before the performance began my mother appeared dangerously pale. As I came down to her at the end Mum beamed at me, her face glowing. "Thank you! Oh thank you for bringing me!"

In the face of old age, illness and irretrievable loss and sorrow, for resilient survivors, the show goes on.

SUMMER, 2012

A PORTRAIT IN TIME

As a little girl, I was fascinated by a portrait on our living room wall. The elegant woman in the portrait seemed out of place in our shabby apartment. I loved to look at this portrait which, I later learnt, was an enlargement of a photograph my mother's sister hid in her underwear during the course of the Second World War. It contained the profile of a regal-looking lady whose long thick hair was swept back, revealing a swan-shaped neck and bare alabaster shoulders. The lady had high, wide cheekbones, and a strong, confident jaw. Pearls hung from her ears, as if in suspended animation, and her almond-shaped eyes stared vacantly into a future she wouldn't live to see. While I studied the portrait, my mother studied me.

"Who is she, Mummy?"

My mother answered sadly. "She's your grandmother."

I was shocked. "She can't be my grandmother! Grandmothers are old!"

The pain in Mummy's sigh was palpable. "My mother never got a chance to get old." Together we contemplated the portrait.

"Her name was Natalia. She was my mother. That makes her your grandmother."

"But she doesn't look like you."

Under the spell of her mother's image my mother's smile was sudden, and sweet. "No. She looks like you."

I searched the portrait for a resemblance to my innocent face, and couldn't find any. "I don't look like her! She's beautiful, and I'm ugly!"

"What?!" Now it was my mother's turn to be shocked. "Where did you get such an idea?"

"Well, when you look at my face you get sad, so I figured it has to be because I'm ugly."

"*Slodka*, sweetheart, you can see that when I look at your face, I feel sad?"

I nodded. Mummy snapped into alert. "*Slodka!*" She insisted, "My mother was beautiful, and so are you. You are beautiful in the same way she was, and when I look at your face I see her beauty in it. That's why I feel sad."

I forced myself to face my mother's pain. "You get sad because you miss her, right?"

"That's right."

"Then you don't think I'm ugly?"

"No no. Of course not."

"But how can I look like your mother when she was a lady, and I'm just a little girl?"

"*Slodka,*" my mother was adamant. "My mother is who you are going to look like."

In Warsaw on the morning of September 1, 1939, my mother was setting the kitchen table for a celebratory breakfast. It was Natalia's forty-sixth birthday. She had been widowed six months before. On a wonderfully sunny morning, without a cloud in sight, my mother heard what sounded like a loud storm. The skies darkened suddenly. Within an hour the windows of Natalia's luxury apartment on Krolewska Street were shattered, and she was huddling against her bedroom wall with her two daughters curled under her arms. The bombardment of Warsaw had begun. So had the Second World War.

September 1, 1939 would prove to be Natalia's last birthday. Within a month, Natalia and her children were homeless. Before the end of the year, they would be refugees. Natalia fell victim to the war's first epidemic of typhus and, with my mother beside her, died in a Russian-run hospital on the evening of New Year's Day, at the dawn of 1940.

The year I was thirteen, my mother took me to a photography studio to have my picture taken. Mum put me through this ritual every few years. Shortly after she made her first trip to Israel, where she discovered relatives on her mother's side. They presented her with a photograph she hadn't known existed. It was a picture of a younger Natalia, as Mum had never known her. She is facing the camera, with her head tilted to one side. Her hip-length hair hangs loose. She wears no jewellery. Her hands are folded demurely over her crossed knees. Her mouth is closed, with a mere hint of a smile. There is a wistful expression in her eyes, which do not look directly into the camera, but look shyly away.

When Mum came home, she brought this faded and scratched photograph to the same photographer who had recently taken my picture.

He gasped. The picture of Natalia looked like a painting of the picture the photographer had taken of me.

The photographer restored and enlarged this picture, though he was unable to remove one large scratch. It was framed and hung prominently in my parents' living room, along with the cameo-like portrait of the older Natalia.

After my mother was widowed and she moved to a smaller apartment, the younger Natalia still claimed a wall in the living room, while the older Natalia-in-profile was positioned over the headboard of my mother's bed, seeming to gaze down at her sleeping child. She kept vigil on the bedroom wall to the end of my mother's life, and beyond. My mother was granted the chance to get old. When terminal cancer came for her she met it at home, in her bed, with me beside her. On the evening of the first snowfall in 2013 the spirits of three women came together; the grandmother who was dead, the mother who was dying, and their memory keeper, who was being left behind.

Today the two portraits of Natalia perch on my walls, along with portraits of my mother and the photograph taken of me when I was thirteen. When guests come to my apartment the first object they notice is the large portrait of the younger Natalia, which is prominently displayed.

"When was that picture of you taken?" Invariably, they ask. "Shortly after the First World War," I deadpan, with a mere hint of a smile.

WINTER, 2024

THE MAN IN THE RAINCOAT

I must be one of the few North Americans lucky enough to have seen Alan Bates perform on stage twice in a lifetime. The last time was in February of 1996, in Toronto, during a visit to celebrate my nephew's first birthday. (I would later discover that my nephew and Sir Alan shared the same birthday.) Bates was playing the master builder in Ibsen's play of the same name. In a Montreal newspaper I'd read a review of the production at *The Royal Alexandra Theatre* in Toronto. Excitedly I called my brother, who resides there.

"Please get me a ticket."

Over the phone line, I could envisage my brother's crooked grin as he dryly responded, "I've already got two tickets."

The first time I saw Alan Bates was in New York, on Broadway, in the Simon Gray play *Butley*. It was Christmas time of 1972. My birthday is in early December. In my native Montreal, the date generally heralds winter's first blizzard. My dad would quip that I took the world by storm. It was cold comfort. I could never hold a party because no one would come.

Once they could afford to, my parents transformed disappointment into joy. A new tradition began. As a teenager, my birthday present became an excursion to New York during the Christmas holidays to catch the British imports on Broadway. I grew up pining over the posters in BOAC display windows. At the time, going to New York to see the British productions was as close as I could get to the London theatre. For my seventeenth birthday, I chose to see Alan Bates in *Butley*.

During the Christmas season of 1972, my mother and I went together to New York. We saw the play. A few days later – it must've been a Wednesday, because the matinee performances were letting out – we were returning to our room at the Piccadilly Hotel on 45th Street, lugging sacks of hard-cover volumes we'd bought at the book shop *Brentano*. We passed a cluster of fans crowded around Paula Prentiss and Richard Benjamin, who were backed against the stage door of the theatre they were performing in, cheerfully signing autographs. Under the light of the stage door at the *Morosco,* next to the hotel we were staying in, HE was standing, draped in the same raincoat his character wore onstage. The atmosphere was damp. There was a drizzle. Bates was in conversation with two men. They weren't fans. They spoke with English accents, and were either friends or colleagues. The matinee crowds continued to pour out of adjacent theatres. Everyone ignored the man in the raincoat. If someone did stop to ask for an autograph, it would be for the Benjamins.

Nervously I nudged my mother. "Oh Ma! Ma!! Look!" She looked. "No! Don't look! Oh Mummy!"

Mummy grinned. "Wanna meet him?"

"Well yeah! But I can't! I couldn't! I don't know how! Maaa!" How do you ask a god for his autograph?

My mother knew how. She strode up to the man in the raincoat and demanded, "Mr. Bates, I want your autograph!" The man in the raincoat seemed annoyed. Cowering at the edge of the wide sidewalk, loaded down with books, I wanted nothing more than for a manhole to open and swallow me up.

The man in the raincoat asked my mother for a pen. My mother didn't have a pen.

"Don't YOU have a pen?" She challenged.

The man in the raincoat seemed to be growing more annoyed. The nerve of this woman interrupting my conversation to demand an autograph and not even supplying her own pen. One of the men fished in his pockets, and found a pen. I recall rain rolling down my cheeks, in lieu of tears. There was thunder in my head, and lightning in my heart.

Slit-eyed, the man in the raincoat peered at my mother. "Now what would you like me to write on?"

It was at this moment that my mother deliberately turned downstage towards the street and declared, "SHARON!" Be still, my heart. "Give me something to write on!"

Alan Bates blinked and looked past my mother, at me. This was the Alan Bates of *Georgy Girl* and *The Fixer* and *Far From the Madding Crowd*. This was the impeccable English actor who'd gone to the top London drama school I dreamt of getting into; this was the emerald-eyed British film star with the shaggy mane of raven hair, and at this instant, he was looking at me. Suddenly calm, I bent down and selected Volume II of Shaw's *Collected Letters (1898-1910)* from one of the two *Brentano* bags filled with books. My mother moved towards me, I moved towards her, and we met in the middle of the wide sidewalk. I handed the book to her and retreated to my post beside the bag. Alan Bates was gazing pensively. At me. I was a very young, shy, and wholesome seventeen. Hmmm... Bates' gaze shifted back to my mother, and his irritated expression melted away. At the corner of one side of his mouth, a camera lens might've picked up a hint of the beginning of a smile.

My mother handed him the book. His gorgeous green eyes dilated and he protested, loud enough for me to hear. "Shaaaw?! I cawn't write on Shaaaw!"

My mother insisted. "Well it's all I've got!"

Reverently the actor turned the front and back pages of the volume, searching for a blank space where his signature wouldn't interfere with the prose of a writer he seemed to consider a god. He found it; he signed and handed the book back to my mother. Then Alan Bates again shifted his gaze and smiled fully, affectionately, kindly and warmly – at me.

Two days after Christmas in 2003, I heard the news of his death. I read that the lights on Broadway and in London's West End were dimmed and a moment of silence observed for the English actor whom the queen had knighted at the start of the year, and whom cancer would kill before the year's end.

Sadly I pulled the Shaw volume off a bookshelf and studied a back, almost blank page which says nothing more than *Best Wishes, Alan Bates.* I put the book away. Then I went downtown, to visit a museum. Perusing the exhibits, I fell into conversation with a teacher from upstate New York who was visiting with her young son. They were spending the holidays museum-hopping in Montreal.

When I left the building, it was drizzling. I opened an umbrella, turned down to a main street and meandered past the festive display windows. The mother and son I'd met at the museum, the light rain and the holiday shoppers frantically spending and frenziedly lugging along the wide sidewalks sacks filled with purchases evoked a ghost of Christmas past. Wistfully I recalled the Christmas season of 1972, once more encountering a god-like actor who was now dead, and not yet seventy.

In 2001, excitedly my mother called me. At her neighbourhood cinema she had just seen the recently released film *Gosford Park.*

"Oh Sharon! I saw a movie! It's for you! It's just for you! All that British stuff that you love! Oh sweetheart! How can I tell you?!" Meaning, how can I describe what I saw. "What can I tell you?!" Succinctly, Mum summed up. "I can tell you only two words – Alan Bates and Maggie Smith!"

These two words I understood completely. These were two magic words. "Alan Bates and Maggie Smith? I'm on my way! I'm in!"

Mum took me to see the movie she had seen only days before. It would be the last film in which Bates appeared. As I watched, Mum watched me. A moment came when Bates, as a stiff, prim and proper butler, allows himself to release a smile. With pleasure, in recognition, Mum and I smiled at each other. In that moment, seeing that smile, twenty-nine years later, we remembered.

WINTER, 2004

OPEN HEARTED

It was bitter, the winter of 1959. An epidemic of Hong Kong flu raged through the city. The disease felled Mum, Daddy and me. We were compelled to quarantine. Who would take care of my infant brother Michael? My mother's sister and her husband weren't an option. My father's siblings couldn't be trusted with anything. Through a network of neighbours, a woman was located on Goyer Street. Her name was Katarina Trautmann. In an audacious dash for freedom, *Herr* and *Frau* Trautmann, with their two teenage daughters, escaped East Berlin in 1953.

Katie Trautmann was born in Aachen in 1912, one of four daughters. There may have been a little brother who died. In 1916 her father was killed on a battlefield in France. Their widowed mother raised Katie and her sisters. In the 1930s Katie was working as a maid in a wealthy home in Berlin. Friedrich Trautmann was a guest. That is how they met. In Berlin, Friedrich Trautmann was an engineer and during the war was recruited as an officer into the *Wehrmacht*. According to what he told Mum, during the war he held a position and was posted to a place where he would not have participated in atrocities, but he was aware that atrocities were being committed. After the war he was considered skilful enough to be of value to the Russians, who conscripted and transported him to the Soviet Union where, for two years, he served a form of slave labour. In Montreal, Friedrich Trautmann earned a modest living as a mechanic.

The Trautmanns' eldest daughter, Helga, was born in 1938. Doris was born on December 8, 1940. I always remember Doris' birthday because it is two days after mine.

In the depths of winter, at the start of 1959, the Trautmanns sheltered and cared for my baby brother Michael. Katie

Trautmann grew to love my brother like the son she never had. She rocked him and held him to her ample breasts and placed him in a carriage positioned in front of a sunlit window, as if he were a plant. When my parents recovered and were once more able to care for Michael, reluctantly, Mrs. Trautmann returned him.

Two years later an apartment across the hall from the Trautmanns' apartment became available, and we moved to 2975 Goyer Street apartment fourteen Montreal Quebec! I had to memorize this address in case I got lost.

"If you can't find your way home, then you go and find a policeman." Mum instructed. "The policeman is your friend. He will bring you home."

I recall our first evening in the new apartment. I was five years old. Mum was on her hands and knees, scrubbing the floor of the room that, for the next seven years, I shared with Michael. Mrs. Trautmann lugged a mop and a bucket. She was helping; scouring and cleaning the adjacent floors. As I watched the two women it seemed to me that I must do my part, so I fetched my toothbrush, filled a cup with water, sloshed the water onto the floor, plopped onto my hands and knees, and began scrubbing away with my toothbrush. Monkey see; monkey do!

Mum stopped scrubbing in mid-scrub. Mrs. Trautmann's mop stopped moving.

"*Slodka.*" Mum whispered. Then she translated. "Sweetheart."

"*Kinde.*" Mrs. Trautmann agreed. Almost in unison, they appealed. "Don't help."

Mum and Mrs. Trautmann spoke German to each other and English to me. They never addressed each other by their first names. Forever formal, the two Europeans called each other "Mrs. Zajdman" and "Mrs. Trautmann".

While Mum and Dad worked, Mrs. Trautmann greeted us at lunchtime with sometimes hot and always lovingly prepared meals. I recall coming home in winter to steaming bowls of chicken noodle soup. Often we had chicken noodle soup because it was Michael's favourite. I also recall sandwiches of linseed bread lined with thin slices of spicy German salami.

After school the door to our apartment, and to Mrs. Trautmann's, was always open to us. Michael grew so attached to Mrs. Trautmann that he began telling people she was his grandmother. He felt guilty about doing so, but wasn't sure why. Instinctively he knew not to repeat this to Mum. Instead, Michael confessed to me. I heard his confession, and then pronounced, "That's not the way it works."

"But I want a grandmother! Why can't I have a grandmother?!"

"Because! A grandmother is a mother who is your mother's mother or your father's mother, except that Mummy doesn't have a mother and Daddy doesn't have a mother, so you can't have a grandmother. Anyway, we've got a grandmother. She's hanging on the wall."

"You mean the lady in the picture? But she's not real."

"Well, she used to be in real. In 'Before The War' she used to be real."

The term "Holocaust" was not yet in common usage, but I had heard of The Land of Before The War. It was a mysterious place my parents returned to when they spoke in Polish.

Michael refused to accept a photo facsimile. "But I want a real grandmother now!"

"Look." My little brother was cute, but he could be exasperating.

"We have our parents but they don't have theirs. So who should cry; them or you?"

"Oh! I never thought of it that way."

Over Jewish holidays, unless Daddy was called upon to lead a Seder, we were never invited to extended family, but we always shared Christmas with the Trautmanns. Their Christmas tree was our Christmas tree. On Christmas Eve, Michael was accorded the honour of sticking the star onto the top branch of the *Tannenbaum*.

"Allez h-up!" Mr. Trautmann would hoist Michael and lift him level to the top of the tree. Nervously Michael fumbled among the decorations, until he managed to insert the star-shaped piece of foil onto a top branch.

"Bravo!" Mr. Trautmann declared, while Mrs. Trautmann applauded. "You did this *gut*!" Michael would thrust out his little chest and beam with pride. Then he'd be lowered back down onto the ground.

I would profit by this greeting card moment by sneaking a piece of chocolate from an open box on the coffee table. Invariably Mrs. Trautmann caught me at it. "Sharon! You will get fat! You want to be an actress! You must have *disziplin!* You cannot be fat!"

"*Ach* Katie!" Generally silent, Mr. Trautmann sprang to my defence. "It's Christmas! Leave the child alone!" Like my daddy, Mr. Trautmann was on my side.

My recollections of Helga are vague. Early she married a German businessman named *Herr* Lothar and returned with him to Germany. Helga looked like a sun-kissed Rhine maiden, but Doris was dark, and looked like Romy Schneider. She had a brief first marriage to a man named *Herr* Apfel. Michael and I called him Mister Apples. Mister Apples worked in a chocolate factory. I thought Doris was wondrously lucky to be married to a man who worked in a chocolate factory! He brought us samples, and Mrs. Trautmann stressed their quality. These were no adulterated Oh Henry bars.

"Kinder, das ist DEUTSCHE Schokolade!"
    I was sad when Doris left Mister Apples. There would be no more *schokolade*.
    I was born slightly lame. From Germany Mrs. Trautmann imported, or perhaps it was Helga who sent over Franz Joseph *Wasser*. Mrs. Trautmann believed this spring water had healing properties. Nightly, either Mrs. Trautmann or Mum would massage my feet with the emperor's elixir, and then they had me walk up and down the living room floor with pencils between my toes. Each evening I had to walk up and down the living room floor with pencils between my toes until, for me, from Germany, Mrs. Trautmann imported the first of Dr. Scholl's arch-supported wooden sandals. In the hours after school, after I finished my homework and before my parents came home, Mrs. Trautmann taught me to knit, and later, to crochet.

In summer, we were invited to the Laurentian Hills, to a place the Trautmanns called their farm. We were welcome to stay all summer.
    There were no animals on this farm. It was a primitive property. There was no indoor plumbing. Walking distance, there was an outhouse. A column of wax paper dipped in honey dangled from a hook on the ceiling over the table used for dining. Flies died there. Still, like kamikaze pilots, more kept flying through the open door off the porch, heading directly for the honeycombed column. I was struck by how stupid flies must be.
    The bedrooms were located on an upper floor. The room I came to think of as mine had a slanted roof. It leaned in as if wanting to speak to me. On soft summer nights, tucked under a light quilt listening to jiminy crickets singing in the tall grass outside an open window, I felt cocooned in a fairy-tale.

On the shore of a nearby lake, wearing nothing but a sunhat and an undershirt, Michael would squat, scoop sand into a pail, and then he'd toss it out again. With floating devices strapped to our waists and Michael clinging to my hand, we'd be guided into the shallows of the lake where we'd splash and cool off. In nearby woods, in August, we'd pick berries that Mrs. Trautmann baked into late-summer pies. I noted that my little brother's eyes were the same colour and shade as the berries, so I came to call him Blueberry Eyes.

With Michael and I ensconced on this oasis, my parents were free to take a break, even if they couldn't afford a full-blown vacation. They scheduled a three-day getaway, but couldn't see it through. After forty-eight hours alone together my mother wailed, "Oh Abram! I miss the kids!"

"OK." Daddy conceded. "Let's go." They got into the family Chevrolet, whose doors against the back seats were sealed so that Michael and I could never fall out, and took off for the Trautmanns' farm.

"Oh. Hi Mummy." Michael and I were perched on a hill within yelling distance of Mrs. Trautmann's country kitchen, companionably sculpting mud pies. "What are you doing here?"

"Oh!" Mum threw herself on me. Ruefully, Daddy shook his head. "Oooo Mummy!" I protested and wriggled out of her embrace. "You're going to make yourself all muddy!"

"*Kinder!*" From down the hill, Mrs. Trautmann trilled. "*Kom!* We have lunch!" Michael and I dropped our inedible pies and got up, mud dripping from our fingertips and, in Michael's case, smeared across his cheeks and chin.

"You better wash your face before Mrs. Trautmann sees you." I warned him.

"I have to go inside to wash my face and Mrs. Trautmann will see me but it doesn't matter!" Michael responded logically, secure in Mrs. Trautmann's unconditional love.

We headed down the hill, trailing mud, while our parents trailed behind us. Mum was sniffling. Daddy had his arm around her.

"What's the matter with you, Mummy?"

"Nothing!" Mum blasted. I'm just so happy to see you, that's all!"

The offspring of Holocaust survivors tend to fault their parents for supposedly viewing them as replacements; surrogates for children cherished and lost. As an officer in the *Wehrmacht*, Mr. Trautmann didn't see his younger daughter Doris for the first four and a half years of her life. When he returned from the front, he was a stranger to her. As a child, I sensed that Mr. Trautmann identified me with Doris. During my formative years, Mr. Trautmann seemed to see me as a second chance. For a former *Wehrmacht* officer, it was fitting that redemption came in the form of a daughter of Holocaust survivors.

Bewildered as he was, my little brother perceived something significant. This middle-aged German couple served as surrogates for the grandparents their war stole from us. Unstintingly they shared their homes, their holidays, and their hearts. Together Mrs. Trautmann and I watched and loved *Lucy*. While massaging my feet with Franz Joseph *Wasser*, Mrs. Trautmann regaled me with the tale of Doris Day, whose original name was Doris Kappelhoff and who, as a teenager, with therapy and exercise, overcame a serious leg injury and went on to sing and dance in the movies. Excitedly, she also told me about a hot new German film star who was taking Hollywood by storm. Because this actor had a name that could be played with, I called him Max The Million! (Though he was born in Vienna and raised in Zurich, for Katie Trautmann, Maximilian Schell was German.)

While Katie Trautmann prepared my meals, monitored my intake of chocolates, and focused on strengthening my feet, my Jewish survivor aunts played cards, went to their hairdressers, and bad-mouthed my mother for placing her children in the care of a woman they referred to "a Nazi bitch".

Decades later, shortly after both our birthdays, in front of a downtown Christmas display window I ran into Doris. She had married again. Her second husband was a Jewish divorcee with five children. Mrs. Trautmann was now step-grandmother to five Jewish children.

In front of a Christmas display window Doris stunned me by saying, "It must've been hard on your mother, having my mother take care of you." Sincerely, with all my heart, I was able to tell her, "No. It wasn't. Mum was grateful that we didn't have to become latch key kids. We couldn't depend on extended family. Because of your mother, we had someone to whom we could come home."

SUMMER, 2020

WHAT'S IN A NAME

I was five years old and in love with Dr. Kildare. Whenever I'd see him, I'd wrap my soft, pudgy arms around our TV set and give his screen image a great, loud smooch. "I love you, Dr. Kildare!" I'd announce, to the silent living room. "I love you!" My mum was just outside the room. She must've been listening.

I had a steady Saturday night date with Dr. Kildare. He was on TV every Saturday night between 7:30 and 8:30, though we were allowed only half an hour together. At eight o'clock, precisely at the time of the program's second commercial, I had to go to bed.

Coming up to one Saturday night, my mother informed me that I would be allowed to stay up until 8:30, so that I could have a full hour with Dr. Kildare. I was thrilled. I did not yet realize that Mum had an agenda.

At 8:30 on Saturday night, as the weekly program came to an end, I saw something I had never seen before. The TV screen filled with two columns of names which I couldn't yet read. Out loud, Mum read them for me, and to me. "Dr. Kildare... Richard Chamberlain... Dr. Gillespie... Raymond Massey..." What did this mean?

"Sweetheart," Mum broke it to me gently. "Dr. Kildare isn't real. He's a character played by an actor named Richard Chamberlain."

I was gobsmacked. Dr. Kildare wasn't real? I looked to my mum for an explanation. "What's a (sic) actor?"

Patiently, Mum explained. "An actor is a person who pretends to be someone else. When he's very good at it, he gets to be on TV."

"No!"

"Yes." I gazed into my mother's sad and haunted eyes. It appeared she was telling the truth.

"But why do they have two different names?" My five-year-old world view had just been shattered. I couldn't keep pace with this turn of events.

"They don't have two different names. Richard Chamberlain is an actor who is pretending to be a doctor called Dr. Kildare."

I stared at the two columns of names scrolling relentlessly down the screen. I was discombobulated.

"This means that everybody on TV is an actor with his own name who is pretending to be somebody else with a different name?"

"Yes, *slodka.*" On uttering this term of endearment, Mum slipped into her mother tongue. "They call it 'credits. The credits.' "

This was far too much information. Yet a glimmer of understanding was beginning to peek into my five-year-old mind. The same person with two different names pretending to be someone else. This was not a foreign concept. Not to the family I was born into.

"You mean like a 'war' name? Like the way some people who knew you in the war call you Krystyna?" My mother's name wasn't Krystyna. A Jewish female was never called Krystyna.

Mum flinched. "Yes, *slodka.* Something like that." A five-year-old child isn't supposed to know about war names. When I asked Mum about her other name, she told me it was her middle name, yet no one called Mum Krystyna except for a few people who'd known her during the war. There was no name for them, then. Today, we call them Survivors. It's a fitting description. Though I became an actor, it was my mother who had gotten so good at pretending to be someone else that she survived.

WINTER, 2023

DON'T ASK

When I was small, with fascination I watched as my father's sister Cesia washed dishes. In a short-sleeved blouse, she'd plunge her arms into sudsy water. There were little blue numbers on the inside of one of her arms. I thought the water would wash them off, but it didn't. I didn't ask my aunt why she had blue numbers on her arm; I asked my mother.

"Auntie has a bad memory. She writes her phone number on her arm so she won't forget it." Genocide taught Mum to be a quick and clever liar.

"But the numbers don't come off! What happens if she moves?!" A woman who had outwitted the Gestapo had no answer for me. When Mum was stumped, she'd change the subject. When Mum was stumped, I'd allow her to.

A year later, we were gathered at my aunt's kitchen table when my little brother blurted, "Auntie, how come you got little blue numbers on your arm?" The adults sat in shocked and embarrassed silence. I kicked my brother under the table.

"Shashi!" The oblivious tyke inserted a second foot into his already crowded mouth. "Why do you kick me under the table?! What did I do?"

The adults were stunned. Their hurt and haunted eyes focused on me. The spectres that lived in the world behind their eyes rose up in my relatives' irises to silently question me. How does the child know? How can the child know? We couldn't protect the children. Can't we protect them, even now?

"*Slodka*, sweetheart." My mother became uncharacteristically gentle. She placed her worn hands on my soft, unmarked arm. "How do you know?"

"I don't know," was my answer to my parents and my relatives and above all, to the ancestors who had risen out

of the ether and were hovering over Cesia's kitchen table.
"I just know we're not supposed to ask."

SPRING, 2019

"NANA"

In the nightmare world of the Warsaw Ghetto there was a half-starved orphan so in love with literature that when the German occupiers banned the act of reading, she became a courier in a clandestine network calling itself a walking library. Risking her life, Renata delivered books to readers. Sometimes she received a tip in the form of a piece of bread, but her payment was that she had access to the books. Literature, always loved, became her weapon against despair. Eerily, hiding in the ghetto, Renata read Fran Werfel's *Forty Days of Musa Dagh*, his account of the Armenian genocide. Crouched in a corner of the room she shared with relatives, Renata began reading Emile Zola's *Nana* – the story of a French prostitute who is the ruin of every man who pursues her. Renata's older brother pulled the novel out of her hands.

"You're too young to read that. You can read it when you're eighteen."

Matter-of-factly the hollow-eyed youngster replied, "I won't live to be eighteen."

Surprising herself, the Jewish girl with the name meaning "reborn" survived. In time she married, and then became a mother. Mine. When I was a little girl, my mother encouraged and guided my reading, gladly feeding my appetite for books. All my English teachers envisaged my becoming a writer – indeed there was one who insisted on it. It was with great solemnity that, one frosty afternoon after school, my mother presented me with a copy of *Anne of Green Gables*.

"When I was your age, I read this book in translation. This book introduced me to Canada. When I was your age my vision of Canada was of a faraway, peaceful land filled with snow. I could never have dreamed that one day my very own daughter would be Canadian-born and I would be giving her this book in the original English."

The entire Anne series had been on my mother's walking library list. *Anne of Green Gables* was her gift to both of us.

My brother's eldest daughter surmounted a learning disability, and became a passionate reader. She would prop up her novels at the table at lunch time, read by flashlight in bed, hide with her books in corners of a large family home, and evade visitors in order to escape into the pages of her latest literary voyage.

The evening after my mother turned eighty, we attended my (now) eighteen-year-old niece's high school commencement. Sitting in a gymnasium, witnessing the celebration of carefree teenagers in the serene land of Anne-with-an-E, tears streamed down the cheeks of my niece's "Nana".

Familiar with the interior of my mother's apartment, the concierge of the building in which she lives has dubbed her "The Lady Who Loves Books". The cancer my mother lives with has slowed her down, so she doesn't get to the libraries as often as she would like. When I moved into my mother's neighbourhood in order to be quickly accessible and available for her, I became my mother's walking library. Mum e-mails to me lists of books she wants to read, I fill the orders at our neighbourhood library and deliver them to her apartment. No matter how treacherous the weather, I always deliver.

Yet The Lady Who Loves Books refuses to read to the end of Emile Zola's Nana. She's afraid that if she does, her life will arrive at its end, too.

WINTER, 2012

"DADDY KAYE"

The pellet with the poison's in the vessel with the pestle; the chalice from the palace has the brew that is true…
     Danny Kaye in and as *The Court Jester*, 1956.

On Wednesday, March 4, 1987, seventy-six-year-old David Daniel Kaminsky, known to the world as Danny Kaye, died. Four years earlier, he contracted hepatitis as a result of receiving tainted blood during a transfusion while undergoing heart surgery. Kaye's clown's heart succumbed at four in the morning.

I recall when he was hospitalized. In the dead of winter, at three am, I woke with a start. In order to fill the disturbing silence, I opened a radio just in time to hear the hourly news; "In Los Angeles, Danny Kaye undergoes heart surgery…"

Six weeks later, my father was dead. I'd never known a world without my father, and I'd never known a world without Danny Kaye. They were born six years apart and died four years apart, short of a month, of hearts so full that they burst; both, on a Wednesday. The two men were manifestations of the same spirit.

I first saw Danny Kaye on his weekly television show in the early nineteen sixties. I was eight years old. It was a revelation. Here was someone as warm and fresh and funny as my father. The identification was so powerful that I took to calling him "Daddy Kaye". When I was twelve, my parents purchased tickets for me and my little brother for a matinee of Kaye's one-man show. He was past his prime; on the last of his world tours. No matter. I was entranced by Kaye's dancing fingers, his twinkling eyes, and his witty rubber face. Later, I cut out the program cover and tacked it on the outside of my bedroom's closet door, where it hung for years. Whether I was practising piano or reading in bed, Danny Kaye was always winking at me. Eventually, my mother had him laminated. Today Kaye is perched on the wall above my computer work station.

In the days before streaming, before DVDS and even before video, in my early teens there was a series of old MGM features being screened at a local cinema. Two of the movies being shown were those of Danny Kaye. There was a suggestion box in the lobby. With an assortment of multi-coloured pencils and the forged handwriting of non-existent fans, I demanded more Danny Kaye. I got it, too. I was a creative writer, even then.

On a business trip to Toronto, my father found a recording of the soundtrack to the film *Hans Christian Andersen*, and a double album filled with musical monologues and tongue-twisting patter songs going back forty-five years. My father handed me the records and scratched his head. "*Nu, ein Gott und ein* Danny Kaye." I can still reel off, by heart, the lyrics to *Anatole of Paris* and *Tschaikovsky.*

When I was fifteen, my mother took me down to New York and Broadway to see the musical comedy-drama *Two by Two.* Kaye played the bible's Noah as a beleaguered Jewish patriarch harassed by a demanding God and equally demanding children. Just before the houselights dimmed, over a loudspeaker a disembodied voice intoned, "Ladies and gentleman, there will be a change in the program tonight…" I gripped my mother's hand, and I think I heard her heart stop. An understudy was replacing Joan Copeland, who played Noah's wife. (In real life, Joan Copeland was Arthur Miller's sister.) I released my mother's hand, and we both began breathing again.

At the curtain call, Kaye singled out a young actress in the cast, and brought her downstage to say hello to her parents, who were in the audience that evening.

Two years later Kaye was back in Montreal to receive an award at an Israel bond dinner. Through back channels, my mother wrangled a ticket for me. Imagine, I got to spend an entire evening watching Danny Kaye eat! I also got to attend the kind of function which was one of the prime targets of my father's merciless mockery. This particular evening outdid even his wild satire. It was an Anti-Semite's Delight of boorishness and vulgarity. At the end of the evening, Kaye rose to give what one assumed was going to be an acceptance speech. Instead, he launched into a maniacal impromptu monologue parodying the idiocies of the evening. He was screamingly funny. Everyone was howling so hard that they failed to recognize how savagely they were being insulted.

Two years later, Kaye returned to give a benefit concert with and for the Montreal Symphony Orchestra. I couldn't attend because I was out of town. I got in the same evening, and in the morning read how Kaye had entered from the rear of the Salle Wilfrid-Pelletier auditorium, tossing batons at the two-thousand seat audience. And I missed it.

I have thought it would be interesting to compare notes with Danny Kaye's daughter. People would tell me what a riot it must be to live with my father. They did not perceive the underlying fury which fuels great satire, nor that this radiant form of outrageousness is also a form of transcendence. The difference between a village idiot and a court jester is awareness, and these two jesters were shrewd enough to mask their brilliance in controlled lunacy, knowing that in a mad world, playing the madcap is the most creative way of staying sane. When I'd be asked what my father was like, I'd answer, "An East European Danny Kaye." The parallel took on poignant irony in the TV movie *Skokie,* when the zany who occasionally took on dramatic roles, here, played a Holocaust survivor.

My paternal grandfather did not have the foresight of Dena Kaye's – or perhaps it was desperation. Mine was a merchant in Poland; hers was a tailor who'd emigrated from the Pale. My grandfather stayed in Eastern Europe and most of my ancestors were murdered there. When Kaye's father was becoming a star on Broadway, mine was hiding in Central Asia. They entered each other's orbits but once, at an Israel Bond Drive in 1949, when the refugee from Hitler's Europe approached the American entertainer and shook his hand. Struggling to carve a new life in a new land, my father shortened it, but he left my mother, my brother and me the legacy of laughter. It is the same legacy his American counterpart left to the world.

My father wasn't famous, and the only celebrity he knew was as a Pied Piper to his children and their friends. When David Kaminsky died, I fantasized that when he reached the place my dad called The Other Side, Abram Zajdman was waiting at the gate to shake his hand, and this time he would be recognized as a kindred blithe spirit, and a chorus of jiving angels would be snapping their fingers and flapping their wings, while Louis Armstrong wailed on his trumpet as rapturously as he did in the film *The Five Pennies,* and what mischief and merriment there promised to be as these two saints went marchin' in.

SPRING, 1987

UPSETTING SANTA

When I was a child, the largest parade in North America was the Eaton's Santa Claus parade. Eaton's was a department store of legend, akin to Harrod's in London and Macy's in New York, except that Eaton's had branches across Canada. Children applied to march in the parade, sometimes waiting years until they were chosen and in danger of not being considered children anymore.

Held in late November, first in Toronto, always on a Saturday morning, the floats and costumes were then transported by train to Montreal, where the parade resumed the following Saturday morning. The spectacle was televised on both the English and French networks, and CBC radio dramas broadcast Santa's perilous flight from the North Pole. In later years imitators would turn up in markets and malls, but everybody knew that the REAL Santa Claus was the Santa Claus who was hosted by Eaton's.

After the parade, Santa was installed on a red velvet throne that matched his red velvet suit, in a private room set aside especially for such a grand personage. The arms and frame of his throne were painted Fool's Gold.

A leafless, silver-branched tree studded with winking white lights twinkled beside him. A court photographer hovered in the background. Santa's Helpers stood sentinel, armed with multi-coloured lollipops. These helpers wore mossy green tights, green suede tunics, and on their heads perched floppy green caps topped by white pompoms. We were told these creatures were elves, yet they bore a marked resemblance to teenagers from local high schools moonlighting on a Saturday morning.

When the stage was set and the fantasy characters in position, a rope serving as a partition was lifted, and a swarm of exhilarated children raced into the enclosure. Me and my little brother were two of them. Like most of the mob we came with, we were accompanied by a parent. In our case, it was our dad.

Excitedly, we stood in line with our peers. We knew that when the time came to address Santa, we were expected to ask him for a Christmas gift. What could we ask for? We were Jewish, and didn't keep a Christmas tree. There was no chimney, let alone a fireplace installed in our small apartment. How could Santa reach us? Where would he make his delivery?

The children who stood in line with us were casually attired, but my brother and I were dressed up and immaculately groomed for what we considered a major event. I wore a blue dress with a blue and white bordered collar and patterned stripe down the middle. A black band held thick chestnut-coloured hair off my high forehead, and my softly-textured, snow-white cardigan was spangled with golden butterfly appliqués. But it was my little brother Michael who rivaled Santa in the colour and originality of his outfit. Michael was resplendent in scarlet red leggings, a matching red, white and blue hockey sweater with the logo of the Montreal Canadiens proudly emblazoned and promoted on his little chest, and to top off the ensemble, he sported a red, white and blue cap on his golden, crew-cut head. Go, Habs, Go! As we drew closer to the front of the line, nervously Little Michael turned to Dad.

"What do I do when I get to Santa? What should I say?"

Instantly, Dad deadpanned, "Tell the guy you want cold cash."

I frowned. My big brown eyes narrowed as I peered at Dad. I wasn't sure this was a good idea, but Little Michael took Daddy at his word.

As a teen-aged elf removed a rope, handed us fistfuls of

lollipops – which Michael handed over to me to hold – confidently he approached Santa's throne and greeted him.

"Hello!" Michael beamed.

"Hello, little boy." Santa's returned Michael's greeting. "How are you."

"I'm fine. How are you?"

It was hard to tell under his rug of beard and bushy white eyebrows, but Santa seemed taken aback.

"Ahh, what would you like for Christmas, little boy?"

Guilelessly, Michael grinned and carried out Daddy's instructions. "I want cold cash!"

Pouf! A hot white light flashed and popped. The photographer hired by Eaton's was taking a picture of us with Santa, a copy of which Dad would have to pay for with cold cash.

Santa spluttered. He was speechless. He looked to our dad. As sweetly as his son, but not so guileless, Daddy smirked. "Ho ho ho!" He winked at the discombobulated dispenser of gifts. "Meeeerry Christmas!"

WINTER, 2023

TUESDAY'S CHILD

I love Christmas trees. I so love Christmas trees that every December, I visit the Montreal Museum of Fine Arts just to look at their seasonal exhibition of trees from around the world.

My earliest Christmas memories include a tree. As a toddler, I didn't know that the tree in our home had been placed there for Miss Jane. Miss Jane was our half French-Canadian, half-Irish nanny. She lived with us and took care of my little brother and me while our parents were at work. When Miss Jane left, so did the tree. I was confused. I asked my dad what had happened to our festive fir. He teased, "I'll get you a Hanukah bush." I remained confused. There's no such thing as a Hanukah bush.

After Miss Jane's departure, we shared a Christmas tree with the Trautmanns, who lived across the hall. In the eyes of a child, there are few sights more splendid than a fully laden *Tannenbaum*. My brother and I would drape the boughs with silver tinsel, and he had the honour of being lifted high in the air to place the shiny star on the top branch.

I was due to be born at Christmas. During a check-up on December 5, the obstetrician informed my mother I was so eager to meet her that it would take but a nudge to coax me into the world. My mother was equally keen to greet me, so I made my entrance during the wee hours of a Tuesday morning on St. Nicholas Day, in 1955. In childhood I imagined myself as Santa's present to my parents – though often I suspected I'd been dropped down the wrong chimney. As I learnt the true meaning of Christmas, as well as the history of my people, I wondered at the irony of the Christian world making such a fuss over the birth of a Jew.

I don't know what the weather was like when I was born. My mother didn't remember, and my father was asleep. Invariably, however, the St. Nicholas Days of my childhood would herald winter's first blizzard. I couldn't have a party because no one would brave the storm. I would gaze forlornly out the window at the whited-out world. My dad attempted to console me. "Sweetheart, you took the world by storm." Then he would serenade me, not with "Happy Birthday", but with a robust, Yiddish-inflected rendition of "Let it snow! Let it snow! Let it snow!"

On my thirty-fourth St. Nicholas Day, my city was assaulted by the horror of a lone gunman murdering fourteen female university students for their "crime" of being women. This tragedy sent currents of rage through me, and shock waves across the country. It is now known as *The Polytechnique Massacre*. For the next decade, if I didn't escape Montreal by nightfall on December 5, something violent would inevitably happen to me.

Getting older feels like climbing a hill. The more distance one gains, the clearer the view.

On my fiftieth St. Nicholas Day, which again fell on a Tuesday, both the weather and the atmosphere were finally, sunny and serene. I never did take the world by storm. I no longer felt the need.

WINTER, 2005

NOT MARY POPPINS

Her name was Jane Houde. She was half French-Canadian, and half Irish. She was born in Quebec City, and raised in a convent there. My parents found her through a newspaper ad. She came to live with us, and to take care of my brother Michael and me while our Mum and Dad struggled to make a living. Dad was on the road. During the week Mum was rooming in a basement in Pointe Claire while running a bakery. Except for Saturday nights, we were alone with Miss Jane. I remember her as sad, quiet, bony-thin, pinched-looking and repressed. She was of an indeterminate middle age, and as plain as her name. She had a brother in Quebec City. She had at least one nephew. Miss Jane was the stereotypical 1950s version of a spinster; isolated and lonely, with nothing in her life except other people's children.

Miss Jane was always correct, and she taught us to be correct. I don't remember hugs and kisses, but I don't remember unkindness, either. What stands out for me is how she taught us to use cutlery. My little brother learned to eat with a knife and fork while still in his high chair. She taught us beautiful table manners. Miss Jane always addressed us as Sharon and Michael, and we always addressed her as Miss Jane. There was no baby talk, and no overt affection, but we felt safe with Miss Jane. When we were able to see our parents at supper on Saturday nights, we would show off what we had learned from our self-effacing nanny.

Miss Jane prepared our meals, and her own. When she mentioned to our German neighbour her quest for fish on a Friday, Mrs. Trautmann informed her that serving fish on Fridays wasn't necessary. Miss Jane grew confused. She had contracted to work for people who came from Poland after the war. Though her charges' parents didn't attend church, the father would drive her to services on Sunday mornings. There was a Christmas tree in the apartment during the holidays. Miss Jane did not realize it had been placed there for her.

When Katie Trautmann from Berlin explained to Jane Houde from Quebec City that fish on Fridays wasn't necessary because her charges and employers were Jewish, the reserved, imperturbable Miss Jane burst into tears.

"But that's not possible! They're wonderful people! And I love the children!"

Katie Trautmann from Berlin, whose husband had destroyed all photographs of himself in *Wehrmacht* uniform, explained to the bewildered convent-raised lady that Jews were as human as she was. Miss Jane had no way of knowing. She had never before encountered a Jew.

Perplexed, Miss Jane said nothing. It was Mrs. Trautmann who related the incident to my parents. They sat down with a flustered Miss Jane.

"Miss Jane, we love you and we're happy with you, but if you feel there's a problem you're free to leave."

"Oh no! I want to stay! I love the children!"

Dad continued driving Miss Jane to church. By his quiet example, the Holocaust survivor re-educated the convent-raised lady.

Miss Jane stayed with us for two years. When my mother was able to move back home she found Miss Jane another position, but our nanny continued to visit. She needed to be slowly weaned away from us as much as Michael and I needed to be slowly weaned away from her.

I was ten years old when I last saw Miss Jane. It was at Eaton's department store, before Christmas. I screamed out her name, ran to her and threw my arms around her. She appeared embarrassed, yet pleased.

I am now older than Miss Jane must've been when she was taking care of us. I too, am single and childless, yet my life bears no resemblance to the truncated existence of an unpartnered woman produced by Duplessis' Quebec. I was not taught to fear the unknown. I was not raised to hate the unseen. I was raised to be free.

Still, my affection for Miss Jane remains. I wonder how long she lived, and how and when she died. I hope there was someone, at the end of her life, who took care of Miss Jane as decently as she took care of me, at the start of mine.

———————

WINTER, 2006

THE SHOW MUST GO ON

It was the dead of winter. It was Saturday morning. In the afternoon I was scheduled to perform in a Children's Theatre production at Victoria Hall. The drama queen in me is tempted to declare that a storm was raging but truth be told, the blizzard had passed. Our cosy corner of North America was transformed into a dark and deserted region of mountainous snow.

The *métro* system did not yet exist. Neither did snowploughs. The buses weren't rolling. The buses weren't moving. Nothing was moving. Or so it seemed.

My parents and I were huddled around the kitchen table. Breakfast was over, but argument was not. Mum insisted that I stay home.

"Daddy can't take the car. He'll get stuck. No one will show up anyway. You can't go."

I was mortified. "But I have to! If I don't show up, they'll never give me another part!" I stopped short of saying, "And I'll never work in the theatre again!" But I did proclaim, "The show must go on." Our teachers at The Montreal Children's Theatre had taught us that. I was an impressionable little thespian. I was also a quick study.

With the edge of a long silver spoon Daddy pressed a slice of lemon against the inside of his glass of tea. My sense of responsibility made him smile. It also prompted him to rise from the table, enter the hallway, pull on his heavy boots, his warm jacket, and the silly hat with the big floppy ear flaps.

"*Mishigah*! Crazy!" Mum wailed, instantly deciphering the intentions behind Daddy's actions. "Abram! What are you doing!" Mum wasn't asking. "You can't do it." Now Mum made her meaning clear. "You won't make it!"

"Well we can't let the child go by herself! And besides,"

Daddy raised his arm and waggled a forefinger. "The show, it has to go on!"

Daddy was a Polish Jew who survived the war years in Siberia. The prospect of trekking from the Cote des Neiges area to Westmount didn't faze him. He was also an older parent. When I was ten, my daddy was almost fifty. But he was a tough and strong Almost Fifty. Mum was overruled.

In late morning we set out into the empty streets, my small mitted hand resting in Daddy's large gloved hand. What confronted us was a wonderland. Ropes of snow rimmed bare branches like sugar frosting. Caps of snow perched on spiked fences, like ice cream in cones. What looked like white sculptures turned out to be cars buried under snow. Despite the early hour street lamps switched on, as if ignited by an attentive elf.

A gust of wind whistled at the snow, startling it off rooftops. Particles of snow, transformed into silver sequins, pirouetted under the illuminated lamps. Smoke curled out of chimneys in pearl grey and crayoned swirls. Formless clouds smudged the sky. Traffic lights were the only spots of colour in a magical, monochrome world.

Generally I was a chatterbox, but now I knew to conserve my energy and hold my peace. In companionable silence I trudged beside my dad. Sometimes I hiked behind him as he marched through deep drifts, creating a trail for me to follow. I raised my knees high and plunked down my feet in the imprints of my father's footsteps. My feet hurt because my feet were flat, like my daddy's feet. But Daddy didn't complain, so neither did I. When snow banks proved too high, Daddy lifted me over them. When wind currents proved too powerful, Daddy pulled me through them.

It was early afternoon when we reached the invisible border which divides Notre Dame de Grace from Westmount. Curtains of clouds parted, and sunshine tossed a spotlight on a fairy-tale-like castle that rose higher than the surrounding mounds of snow. Through the frost-laced windows of this wondrous Gothic structure I glimpsed chandeliers blazing with light. We were approaching the imposing Victoria Hall.

"Did we make it, Daddy?" Anxiously, I broke our three-hour silence. Are we going to be on time?"

Daddy raised the sleeve of his jacket and checked the face of his wristwatch. A barely perceptible sigh escaped his lips and was caught by particles of frigid air.

I would make it to the dressing room before the two o'clock matinee. So would every other child scheduled to appear on stage that afternoon. The silver metal band of Daddy's wristwatch glittered in glints of cold winter sun.

WINTER, 2009

SOMEONE TO WATCH OVER ME

My aunt Ania owned and operated a dry goods shop. Each year, for Halloween, she created wonderfully elaborate and imaginative costumes for her daughter Eva, and for me. In particular, I recall the black-and-orange quilt with matching cap that carved me into a pumpkin. I had the figure for it. However, the remote October I'm reflecting on, I went trick-or-treating as a gypsy. Aunt Ania sewed a rainbow of chiffon onto a belt, which was attached to the area of my anatomy that, we fervently hoped, would one day whittle down to reveal a waist. I wore a real skirt and tights underneath the belt-load of scarves, to keep me warm on this cold autumn evening. I also wore sturdy Oxford shoes, a sober white blouse, and a red wool cardigan. A red sash, with sequins sewn in, was wrapped around my thick dark hair. With my flashing dark eyes and hair, red was my colour. My daddy said so. Eva, who played in the school band, lent me her tambourine. Eva was going trick-or treating as a prince. The fact that she was a girl was irrelevant. My cousin preferred princely hose to a princess' robe. As a prince, Eva got to wear the mossy green tights she wasn't allowed to wear under her school tunic. Now she wore the tights under a form-fitting forest-green tunic that her mother draped on her. I inspected my cousin's costume.

"You don't look like a prince, you look like Robin Hood."

Eva was taken aback. "Weell, Robin Hood could be a prince."

To me, the line was succession was smudged. "How?"

Disconcerted, Eva dismissed me. "Oh, you're always asking stupid questions!"

When dusk fell a plump little gypsy, a girl-prince and her slave ventured into the dark suburban streets. Rosie was Eva's slave. Her costume was easy. All she needed were chains. Rosie was also an Elvis fan. On Sundays Rosie would recline on my aunt's plush loveseat playing Eva's Elvis records – not the good songs, but the sappy ones that were the soundtracks to those god-awful movies. While Elvis crooned, Rosie would kiss his image on the record jacket and hug and cuddle its cover. She never seemed to care that she was kissing painted cardboard. Rosie would kiss Elvis' picture ON THE LIPS! She knew I was watching her, and she wasn't even embarrassed.

On this Halloween, the prince and her slave carried sacks ready to be filled with edible treats, but all I had was a penny box for UNICEF. My mother made me do it. There was no point asking anything for myself. Even when I managed to come home with a filled sack, Mum would confiscate my loot and hand it over to the children's hospital.

"If chocolate and candy aren't healthy, then why are you giving it to kids who are sick?!" Like my query concerning Robin Hood's claim to the throne, I never got an answer to that, either.

Our motley trio's outing was going well until we turned a corner onto an abandoned street. Our prince had led us there. Eva was the eldest, and she was panic-stricken.

"There's a man following us!" Prince Eva hissed. She was right. A shadow loomed under a street lamp. We stopped. The Shadow stopped. When we started to walk, The Shadow started to walk. We stopped again. So did The Shadow. Rosie wanted to run, but the chains she'd attached to her ankles, as well as to her wrists, prevented her from doing so. I would never try to run because I knew I couldn't run fast enough. Prince Eva and The Elvis Admirer were whipping themselves into a frenzy. I felt oddly calm. There was something comfortingly familiar about the sound of the tired, flat-footed step falling onto the sidewalk behind us.

"I'm going to see who it is."

"No!" Prince Eva started to cry. She stood paralysed. "Don't turn around!"

"Aw, quit balling." The littlest gypsy scolded her older cousin. "This is dumb!"

I turned to confront The Shadow. It's always best to confront one's shadow. My suspicions were confirmed. "Daaaaddy!" I shook the tambourine at my taken-for-granted protector. "You promised! You're not supposed to be here! How could you embarrass me?!"

Caught in the light of the lamp, The Shadow hung his head.

"I didn't want to!" My father fibbed. Or maybe he didn't. My father fostered independence but father, like daughter, was no match for the matriarch. "I'm sorry." Sheepishly, The Shadow apologized. "Mummy made me. You know I can't say No to Mummy!"

AUTUMN, 2005

THE BEST PLAY HE NEVER SAW

When I was twenty and dreaming of becoming an actress, my father and I made our annual pilgrimage to the Shaw Festival. At sixteen I had stumbled upon a tiny ad for the fledgling festival, and the following summer we rode out to the historic border town that had repelled an American invasion in 1812. When we first discovered it, the old Upper Canada fort of Niagara-on-the-Lake, situated on the shore of Lake Ontario twenty-six kilometres from Niagara Falls, was noted more for its prettiness and historical significance than for its cultural life. But when a local wit posted a sign in front of his cottage which read, "Shaw's House", the old fort town hosting the festival came to be referred to, in our house, by the name my father gave it: "Niagara-Falls-on-the-Lake, where Shaw lives."

When I discovered the Festival, the main stage productions were held in the renovated courthouse; lunchtime theatre was housed in the town's original theatre, the Royal George. The large, modern Festival Theatre was about to be constructed, and that's where we saw Kate Reid play the title role in *Mrs. Warren's Profession*. At her first entrance, the audience gasped. A character actress known for her cello-toned voice, alcoholic binges, swollen body and out-sized talent, Reid had whittled down to a shadow of herself. Her large dark eyes, always luminous, seemed to bulge out of her head now. For the moment she was on the wagon, channelling her demons into a performance so searing that it left the festival audience sitting in stunned silence.

A passionate twenty-year-old, I needed no prompting. I leapt to my feet and began to applaud. My father, embarrassed, tugged at the hem of my skirt. Too late. Granted permission, the audience followed my lead. The Festival Theatre audience was on its feet for Kate Reid.

We left the theatre and got into the car. We were staying

in Toronto, which was two hours away. On the steering wheel, my father's hands were trembling. He drove no further than the outskirts of town when he stopped, overcome by what he had witnessed on stage.

"I can't drive that far. I won't make it." Daddy turned the car around, and we rode back to Niagara. It was late September, and nearing midnight. The wind was howling, and mustard-coloured leaves rained to the ground. Queen Street, the main street, was empty and quiet, except for the after-theatre cabaret performing upstairs at The Buttery, and table lamps that glowed through the window of a bistro called Captain Brassbound's. We were the only patrons at Captain Brassbound's. My father ordered a bowl of vegetable soup. When it arrived, he cupped his hands around the bowl to warm and steady them. My loquacious dad had been struck dumb. He lowered his head in contemplation. Steam rose from the bowl. Across the bare wooden table I reached out my hands to his.

"Now do you understand, Daddy? This is what I want to be able to do. It's my dream."

I loved not only the theatre productions at the Shaw Festival, but also the laid-back ambience of the unhurried town. Though, initially, my dad attended the Festival in order to be with me, he soon grew to love it as much as I did. Still, Dad wasn't a hard-core fan. If I arranged to see two productions on the same day, he'd attend the evening performance with me, but pass on the matinee. Instead, he would stretch out under a tree at the edge of the lake. I imagine Dad interrupted his reverie to regularly check his wristwatch. As the time drew near, he would rise and saunter down an increasingly touristy Queen Street in order to meet me at the theatre when the show let out.

One shimmering Saturday in mid-summer, Dad's choice

cost him. He missed the most rollickingly mirthful production I can recall of any season, ever. The actors set off a three-hour laugh fest that had a full house screaming with glee. At five o'clock, as the sun broke through a cluster of clouds, the audience floated through the theatre exits as if on a cloud. Emerging with the throng I could see Dad standing near the main entrance, waiting for me. As I inched my way toward him through the crowd, I saw Dad alert and receptive to the radiant expressions on the faces of audience members. Laughter still rippled through our ranks, and it was impossible not to overhear the glowing remarks.

By the time I reached Dad, he was tsk-tsking with his teeth and vigorously shaking his head. "That's the best play I never saw." Caught off-guard, I took the bait.

"But Daddy, you didn't see it."

"Well that's what I said!" Dad beamed, surprised and delighted to have fooled the one person he felt he couldn't fool. Then he reiterated, rubbing in the punch line, not only for me, but for all who cared to hear: "That's the best play I *never* saw!"

We had already purchased our tickets for the season of 1983 when Dad died suddenly, in early spring. My mother and I decided to honour him by honouring the tickets. It was a bad idea. It was too painful for us to have Mum sitting in the seat we both knew had been intended for Dad. We never went back.

After my father's death, I went to work in the family business with my mother to ensure that my younger brother would finish medical school. I was thirty-five when I finally returned to the pursuit of my youthful dream: working in the theatre. My range had broadened and deepened. Soon I was playing large parts in small venues. At age thirty-eight I was offered a one-woman show. At forty, I played the lead in a play presented in a local auditorium. At the end of the performance the audience sat in stunned silence before leaping to its feet to offer me an ovation. As I was leaving, a woman ran over and grabbed me by the wrists.

"Oh my dear!" she cried. "What a powerful performance! Look at me! I'm shaking! You don't belong here! You should be performing at Stratford! You should be playing at the Shaw Festival! Oh my dear, I'm going to dream about you all night. Look at me! I'm shaking so hard, I don't know how I'll be able to drive home!"

I trembled too, hearing an echo from that autumn when I was twenty. I returned to my apartment by bus, alone. Collapsing onto my bed, I flung my arms over my eyes, yet tears filled them, anyway. In the stillness and the silence I whispered, "Daddy. I did it. That was for you."

WINTER, 2017

AN ANGEL AT OUR TABLE

Aunt Felicia was a sour woman. The only person she showed affection for was my little brother Mikey. It unnerved him. "What's wrong with me? She likes me! She doesn't like anybody but she likes me! What's wrong with me?!" I suspect it went against my aunt's principles to demonstrate her true feelings for her own little brother. As a boy, my dad was a prankster. As a man, he donned the cap of the court jester. Yet each Passover it was my father who led the Seder service, even though it was held in his brother-in-law's house.

Raised to become a rabbi, Dad had turned to socialist rebellion. He could recite the *Haggadah* backwards, forwards, with full expression, and at any speed he chose. One year, Aunt Felicia informed my male cousins that they could be excused from the table to watch the hockey play-offs if the service ended before the game did. Hockey play-off games go on forever – but the Seder service goes on longer. Auntie's mistake was to make this promise within earshot of my father.

At first, the shift in rhythm was imperceptible. Dad began chanting more quickly than usual, and the uncles dutifully picked up the pace. Incrementally, his chanting grew faster and louder and faster still, until he was hurtling through the *Haggadah* at the tongue-twisting pace of a Danny Kaye patter song. Daddy kept his head down, his face straight, and his eyes fixed firmly on the Hebrew text before him. The uncles were forced to follow as best they could. Aunt Felicia fumed in helpless fury. The boys beamed. Before the evening ended, they got to see the last part of the hockey play-off game.

It is the role of the youngest child to open the door for Elijah, prophet, angel, and protector of children, so he can enter the household and drink from the goblet of wine which has been prepared for him. By rights that task should've been performed by my little brother, but when the moment comes for the participants to dip their pinkies into their wineglasses ten times to symbolize the ten plagues which have befallen Egypt – and it comes before the entrance of the angel – my little brother would cuddle up to our mother and merrily dip his pinkie into her wineglass along with her. Whereas our mother would then wipe the residue onto a napkin, like the rest of the grown-ups, Mikey would remove the wine from his finger by licking it off. Ten drops of *Manieschewitz* would knock him out, and he'd spend the rest of a very long evening curled up on our mother's lap, his pudgy palms clasped as if in prayer and pressed against a cheek, his *yarmulke* askew on his flaxen crew cut; a beatific smile on his cherubic face. Thus, the role of gatekeeper fell to me.

"You mean to tell me that he comes to our house and to everybody else's house all at the same time?" I would query, when instructed to stand watch.

"Well he's an angel, he can do that. Except in Israel. In Israel he gets there seven hours later, because of the time change."

As my aunts and uncles and older cousins remained at the long dining table continuing the recitation, I was told when to open the door, I was informed when Elijah finished his drink, and then I was directed to close the front door to my aunt's duplex because Elijah had just made his exit.

"But I can't see the angel!"

"Look harder," urged my father. I squinted my eyes. "I still can't see the angel!"

Daddy smiled his warm, gentle smile. "*Shepsaleh*, you have to look with different eyes."

My big cousins snickered. The entire tribe insisted they

could see Elijah clearly. It occurred to me that if I joined my relatives at the table, I'd be able to see the angel too.

"Why can't I just come back to the table and watch the angel drink the wine? Why can't he let himself out?"

"It's not polite to let a guest leave alone. With an angel, you have to be a gentleman."

I had no answer. Yet.

By the time I was eight, I was fed up with this game. "I don't care if I'm a gentleman or not! After I open the door I'm coming back to the table! I want to see him drink!" I was adamant. Daddy quickly improvised.

"OK. You can come to the table and you will see the angel drink." (Mikey still couldn't hold his liquor.) When cued, I opened the door for Elijah, as I did every year. I marched back to my aunt's dining room table. Maybe I walked behind Elijah, maybe alongside him. If I bumped into the angel, I didn't notice.

I stood among the adults in front of my aunt's long dining room table which held a large, ornate silver drinking vessel filled to the brim with a deep burgundy-coloured wine. The moment of truth had arrived.

"OK." My father instructed. "Watch. The angel's going to drink." I held my breath. My father slipped his knee under the table and shook it. The silver vessel shimmered under the twinkling crystals of the chandelier. Within the confines of the oval-shaped cup, the dark liquid trembled. I lowered my head and peered. "It didn't go down!" I scowled. "When you drink there's supposed to be less in the glass! It didn't go down!"

My father's frustration was beginning to match my own. He pursed his lips, and pointed to the goblet.

"Watch again. The angel's going to drink again!" This time, my father kneed the bottom of the table with such force that the wine spilled over the rim and onto the tablecloth – onto my aunt's snow-white tablecloth with the lace trim which she displayed only on special occasions. Auntie stared in horror at the deep burgundy-hued stain.

I gazed at the goblet in wonder and awe.

"Oh!" Gleefully I clapped my hands, convinced, at long last. "What a sloppy angel!"

Daddy was satisfied. Auntie sat stewing over the ruin of her finest linen. She glowered at her youngest brother. Daddy met her smouldering glare and softly, sweetly, in accented English, he reminded her, "You can't get mad from an angel."

The last Seder my father led was held in his own home. Our last Seder was his last supper. A week later, Daddy was felled by a massive coronary. My mother found him. He was wearing a smile. He had been getting ready to attend a hockey play-off game.

SPRING, 2004

UNTIL WE MEET AGAIN

I identify the month of April with my dad because he was born in April and died in April. Like another rebellious Jew, my father's last supper was a Seder.

My father's favourite colour was green. He identified the colour green with the beauty of nature and the promise of hope and renewal inherent in the coming of spring.

Every time my dad went on a trip, it rained. I identified Daddy's departures with the rain. One afternoon in spring, long ago, I was walking with my dad. Clouds shifted, gathered, swelled with anger, and released a torrent of April showers.

"Daddy?" It dawned on me that I didn't know, but surely my daddy would know. "Where does the rain come from?"

Whimsically, my father responded, "De engels in de heaven are making a party. Dey are getting dronk and trowing down de extra..." Here, he hesitated, and then he chose, "Coca Cola!" These celestial revellers sounded Russian, and Dad had decided to sanitize, for a young audience, his version of The Origins of Rain, by substituting Coke for vodka. Still, the story didn't... ahh... hold water.

"If the angels are throwing down the extra Coke, then how come the rain isn't black?!"

Now Daddy was non-plussed. He halted in his tracks. The man was stymied, and I knew it.

"You can't answer, eh?" I harrumphed in triumph. My victory was short-lived. Like the superb actor he could've become, Dad quickly improvised.

"Waaaalll, maybe its Seven-Up!"

Whether it's composed of vodka or a cocktail of soft drinks, I still enjoy walks in the spring rain.

When we buried my father, it started to rain. By the time we got home from the cemetery, the heavens had cracked open. Thunder roared and lightning split the sky. My mother stared out the window, shook her fist at the horizon, and began to laugh.

"Abram! You just got there and you're starting already?!"

It took a massive coronary to kill a man who seemed like a buoy that kept bobbing to the surface, no matter how many times trouble and hardship pushed him down. He was a Polish Jew who survived the war years in the Soviet Union yet refused to identify himself as a Holocaust survivor, believing that others, especially my mother, had suffered far more. Dad believed in looking forward to the future, and discouraged dwelling on the past. He enjoyed good food, fine wine, and cognac. His reading tastes ran to Soviet espionage memoirs because, I believe, they gave him a context for what he had endured during the war.

Dad disliked being cooped up indoors, and often felt the need for "air". Dad's need for "air", as well as his need for private time and space, took him on long, solitary walks, even during the deep freezes of our Canadian winter. On the easier, early spring walks he'd smile his warm, sweet smile and lift his head to the still-bare branches, welcoming the warbling birds that had returned from southern climes. Profusely he greeted the neighbourhood dogs, and perfunctorily nodded to their owners.

I doubt Dad believed he was invincible, though he tried to give us the impression that he did. There was no self-pity in my father, though there was bitterness and resentment, aimed mainly at the older siblings who removed him from school and sent him to work when he was so close to graduation, after their father died suddenly, before the war, when Dad was fifteen. All his life Dad felt insecure about his lack of formal education. Like the character of Scarecrow in The Wizard of Oz, Dad confused the possession of a diploma with the ownership of a brain and hence, never realized how brilliant he was.

No matter how tough their lot, my mother would reassure my dad, "No one's trying to kill us. We have the children, and we have each other." In my mother my father found the unconditional love, support and acceptance he should've received from his surviving siblings. His wife and kids became his world. He dedicated himself to doing what he had to do in order to ensure that his children could do what they wanted to do.

Dad's sense of fun was infectious. He turned teaching, and learning, and even shopping for groceries into a game.

"I like de yellow epples mit de red chicks! Let's look for de yellow epples mit de red chicks!" To this day, I hunt for the rosiest-cheeked yellow apples I can find. And of course, broccoli looked like trees, and trees looked like broccoli.

Dad's sense of fair play was fierce, and he could carry a grudge to the grave. In order to cope with his often-outraged sensibilities he learned to laugh at everyone and everything. His laugh was infectious, and it was loud. In the best eastern European tradition, often Dad laughed in lieu of crying.

"The world is a beautiful place," he insisted. "It's people who make it ugly." When human nature's ugly side turned its face to Dad, Dad would turn to trees. He didn't hug them, but he would lean against them, lie under them, and donate money to have them planted in Israel. "Making the desert bloom" was more than literal, for Dad. It was also a metaphor.

Dad dreaded the prospect of growing old and getting sick, and he managed to avoid both. Without warning, he dropped like a felled tree. My mother was a youthful fifty-four when she was suddenly widowed. Shattered, she picked up the pieces and reinvented herself as a Holocaust educator. Ultimately, she would be awarded the Order of Merit. Regardless, no one and nothing could fill the void left by Dad. On his thirtieth *yahrseit* she cried, "Thirty years with him, and thirty years without him. Why did he have to leave me so soon?'

My mother would not have to suffer another *yahrseit*. Six months later her long-standing cancer became untreatable, and she would die on the first night of Hannukah, during the first snowfall of the season.

With Dad, there was no warning. With Mum, there was too much. In the last weeks of her life I lay beside my weakening mother. Wordlessly, with waning strength, she would lift her arm and I would curl under it, trembling and terrified, clinging to her like a baby bird snuggled under the wing of its mortally wounded mama. Each evening, after Mum drifted into a drugged sleep, I returned to my apartment to cry a lot, to sleep a little, if I could, to pull myself together and to do it all again the next day. Each evening, as I left my mother's apartment, there was a car parked in front of the building's entrance. Its license plate read DAD, and its logo, as with all car plates in Quebec, read *Je me souviens.* (I remember) The car with the license plate that read DAD sat in front of my mother's building every evening for three weeks.

On the evening of November 27, 2013, on the first night of an exceptionally early Hannukah, I sat beside my supposedly unresponsive mother, reading out loud to her. As the words fell from my mouth and the tears coursed down my cheeks Mum's features softened, and her laboured breathing eased. She looked like an ill child listening to a bedtime story. Her soul escaped her tortured body like a bird flitting from a tree. I cannot tell the precise moment Mum passed, yet I was there. It was that gentle. All I know is that there was a new and sudden stillness in the air. Even more sudden, and stranger still, there was peace.

After Mum stopped breathing and I stopped reading I

kissed her lightly on the forehead and suggested, "Go be with Daddy now. I'll see you – both – soon enough."

An hour later I stepped out of the building, into a night illuminated by the candle-lit *menorahs* in neighbours' windows, and by the moist, doily-like falling snowflakes. The entranceway was clear. The car that had kept vigil during the black, rainy nights of November was no longer there.

WINTER, 2015

HEY MA, LOOK AT ME

During the first week of September I swim in my neighbourhood's outdoor community pool. The day camps have closed, and the children have returned to school. With the children gone and a softer sun beaming on the water and on me, I feel as if I'm vacationing at a resort. There is no ocean on the horizon and there are no waving palm trees, but strangely enough there are gulls wheeling in the clear blue sky. On the outlying lawn butterflies flit onto fuzzy-headed purple clover, bumble bees drone in the background, and the first yellow leaves dive into the water and land at the bottom of the competition-sized pool. I can see them clearly as I propel myself through water warmer than the air, which has a nip in it. I am wearing prescription goggles, which enables me to open my eyes and see underwater as clearly as I did when I was a five-year-old learning to swim. I didn't want to learn. My mother insisted upon it. The first six months of swimming lessons were an ordeal. My mother and I would drag to the YMYWHA by bus in the dead of winter, even in blizzards. It took the good part of half an hour to relieve myself of the layers of clothing and the heavy coat and scarf and hat and boots I was bundled in, in order to get into my bathing suit. A hard plastic cap had to be stretched and fitted over my heavy braids, which placed unremitting pressure on my skull. When I whined about the effort involved my mother would snap, "You are going to learn. One day, you will thank me."

It was when I was squeezed into the bathing suit and bathing cap that the worst part loomed. I had to enter the pool area and climb down a ladder into the water. I was awkward and fat. My swim mates mocked me. The saving grace was our teacher, Paul Rosenthal. I remember his name, and I shall always remember him. He was a German

Jew, a refugee from The Third Reich. I don't know when nor how he escaped, but Paul Rosenthal's survival and entry into my existence set me on a course that saved the quality of my life.

By the time I was placed into my swim teacher's paw-like palms, he must've been in his forties. He was muscular and handsome, with a tenderness that belied his physical bulk. Paul – if memory serves, we called him Paul, not Mr. Rosenthal – paid extra attention and took special care with me. He would stand halfway between one end of the lane and the other and coax; "Just this far, Sharon. Come, come. Swim to me only this far. You can do it. I know you can do it." As I paddled frantically towards Paul, he would surreptitiously back up until he reached the end of the lane. Then he would scoop me into his warm, strong arms and exult, "Look Sharon! Look behind you!" I gasped with surprise and growing confidence when I realized how far I had come. "You see! You swam all the way across the pool!" By spring I had become the star of the class, bouncing on the diving board and shouting across the water, to the outlying stands, "Hey Ma! Look at me!"

My mother was going through anguish of her own, during the winter I learned to swim. Mum had never learned to swim. When she was seven years old her father threw her into a local stream in a practical application of the adage that what doesn't sink, will survive. As Mum started to drown her father's sister fished her out of the water and turned on her brother, cursing him with invectives that were a Polish equivalent of "What were you thinking?!" This violent form of baptism left Mum with a lifelong fear of water. Yet seven years later she would wade through the slime and rat-infested sewers of Warsaw, escaping its infamous Ghetto. For Mum, the ability to swim was equated with survival.

While keeping vigil in the spectator stand of the pool

area at the Y, Mum silently endured the nastiness of the other mothers as they watched me struggling to climb up and down the ladder. My classmates' mothers were as cruel as they were. Ironically, or not, the most vicious of the lot was an obese woman by the name of Mrs. Shulman. All winter Mum cringed as Mrs. Shulman smirked and scoffed at "that spastic fat kid who can't even get herself in and out of the water. She has no business being here. Why does her mother bother to bring her?!" It was only in spring, when I called out triumphantly from the diving board and Mum acknowledged me with a curt nod, that Mrs. Shulman realized who had been listening to her rants. She may have become embarrassed, if she was capable of embarrassment, but from then on Mrs. Shulman bit her virulent tongue. Mum maintained her silence and her dignity, looking beyond the prattling, unaccented women and onto the water, not at me, but at the fellow survivor and refugee who had done for her daughter what she could not. My swim teacher caught the sadness in her haunted eyes and acknowledged Mum's mute gratitude with a slow smile and quiet pride.

Swimming was, and continues to be my salvation. In the years to come I would swim my way through massive weight loss and massive personal loss. From my teen-age years on, when my parents moved us into an apartment building with both an indoor and outdoor pool, I rarely lived swimming pool-less. In the years to come, I would coax my mother into the water and support her weightless body so that she could lean back, let go, and experience what it feels like to trust, float and surrender. On seaside vacations Mum would grip my hands while edging sideways into the ocean in a valiant attempt to conquer her fear of water. She would chatter in order to distract herself, and when a wave rose up and slapped her open mouth I laughed, so that she might laugh, too. Wet, refreshed, and worn out by the challenge she had set for herself, Mum would declare, "That's enough!" and retreat to the shore. As the tide ebbed and the sun set she would sit in the sand gazing, in fascination, as a group of gulls gathered together, seemingly by appointment, and stood at the edge of the water, waiting patiently, we decided, "For Daddy to bring them home."

My mother is gone now. I plunge into the water while dying yellow leaves drop to the bottom of the community pool and lie still there. As I push and propel, my eyes open and my vision restored, I marvel at how it's possible to feel so fortunate, so grateful, and so intensely lonely, all at the same time. Hey Ma, look at me. I'm still swimming. Thank you.

AUTUMN, 2015

MIKEY'S VISION

When my brother's children were small, we would accompany them to the Christmas pantomimes in downtown Toronto. During a performance one winter, a contact lens slipped out of my brother's eye. When we left the theatre he handed the car keys to his wife and informed her, "You'll have to drive us back. I can barely see." I looked up at my brother and smiled. Michael towers over us. He is a gentle giant whom patients call "Dr. Mikey" –who are able to speak, that is. Wee ones recently arrived from the womb into the world communicate by peeing on him.

My brother caught my smile, but didn't understand what provoked it.

"What?" Michael was blank.

My weak, heavy-lidded eyes twinkled behind spectacles.

"Now you know what a Cyclop feels like! You don't have twenty twenty DIVISION anymore!"

My nieces were puzzled. For my brother, a light switched on. He smirked. "You remember stuff like that?"

"Buddy," I was rubbing it in, "I can SEE it as if it happened yesterday."

My brother and I were at a summer camp located in southern Ontario. On a Sunday afternoon in midsummer we were taken by bus on a field trip to Ottawa to visit our parliament buildings. We were at the top of the Peace Tower when my little brother erupted, "Shashi! Look! Daddy's car! Down there! I see Daddy's car! They're here." The future doctor diagnosed the situation. "Mummy and Daddy are here!" Our little lumberjack couldn't pronounce the sound of the letter R and knew he couldn't, so he stopped trying to call me "Sharon" and called me "Shashi" instead. The nickname stuck.

I looked down from the platform of the Tower, onto the streets far below. It was a cloudless summer day. The cars parked along the downtown boulevards shimmered in the heat like brightly painted dinky toys. Though I wasn't yet wearing glasses, it appeared impossible to single out a particular car. Nonetheless my brother pointed and implored, "Shashi! Please. I can see the gween Chevvolay! And you shoes is on the miwwa!" Our father had tied my first cloth baby booties to the rear view mirror. He considered it a good luck charm. We were taught to identify the family car by looking out for the tiny booties dangling from the mirror.

"You can't see that from up here!"

"But I do. Oh why won't you believe me?!" Exasperated, Mikey turned away and tugged on the sleeves of our campmates, insisting, "My mummy and my daddy are here!" Our campmates dismissed him as a pest. I was held responsible.

"Tell your little brother to shut up!" Mikey was hurt.

"Listen Mikey." I put my arms around him. "I can understand that you miss Mummy and Daddy very much, but you know they're at home in Montreal."

"No they're not!" Mikey pouted. "They're here. They're somewhere here! Maybe downstairs!" Mikey's Thinking Cap was firmly set. "Please Shashi, let's go downstairs and find them!"

I knew we couldn't separate from the group and go hunting through the House of Commons for a set of phantom parents. I tried to comfort my little brother, but he was inconsolable.

Our field trip over, Mikey sat silent and sullen, next to me, on the bus. As we rolled down a hill through the camp gates a green Chevrolet, parked in the field next to the flagpole, loomed on the horizon. It seemed to be mocking us. Still, I wasn't sure. If I could just see my baby booties, then I'd be sure.

Mikey didn't need confirmation. Instantly, he went

berserk. "The car! The car!" He bounced frenetically in his seat. "I toll you! I toll you!" He accused our fellow passengers. Before the driver came to a full stop and before I could stop him, Mikey dashed down the aisle, scampered down the steps and pounded on the locked door. He turned his sturdy, stocky torso towards the driver and demanded, "My mummy and my daddy are here! Lemme out!" The startled driver obeyed his command.

Indeed, it appeared our parents were on the site – but where? Frantically Mikey scoured the camp grounds screaming, "Mummy! Daddy! Where are you?!" His cries were answered by the figure of a woman rising out of a lawn chair set by the lake.

"Here we are, sweetheart!" Mum waved. "Abram! Look! It's the kids!" Our dad raised himself from an adjacent chair. For me, the beam on my father's face was like a guiding light.

Our mother flung open her arms, and Mikey raced into them. I could see the top of his platinum-coloured crew cut as he nestled into her enveloping embrace. As I got closer to the shoreline, I could also see two strangers with our parents. Unknown to my brother and me, our parents were entertaining houseguests from overseas. They had given them a tour of Ottawa, and since the camp was located a few miles outside Perth, on the spur of the moment they decided to drop in and surprise us. It was our parents who got the surprise when they entered a summer camp at the height of summer, emptied of its children. The kitchen staff assured them that all was well; we'd been taken on a trip to visit the Parliament buildings, and were due back in half an hour.

What tourist or student group doesn't visit Parliament when taken on a tour of Ottawa? Our parents were showing their guests the Gothic buildings that house our government half an hour after we got there.

The campers and counsellors were dumbfounded. The grown-ups were impressed. So was I. As for little Mikey, he was vindicated. I turned to our campmates and suggested, "I think you should apologize to my brother." Sheepishly, they did. Our parents stared at their tot in admiration.

"But Mikey, how could you see from so far away that it was our car?"

"Hmmmph!" Mikey raised his chin, stuck out his chest, and lifted himself up to his full height – which wasn't yet very high. Proudly, he announced, "I have twenty-twenty DIVISION!"

SUMMER, 2010

INSULT AND INJURY

I sat at the kitchen table, running my tongue around the loosening tooth in my head. Everyone in my class had already lost their first tooth. Everyone had already had their first tooth replaced by the Tooth Fairy with a quarter under their pillow. Everyone, except for Sheree Nudleman, who held court in the schoolyard, and smoked cigarettes. Sheree swore that her real father was Tony Curtis, and he was coming to get her and would take her to Hollywood as soon as he finished his latest picture. Sheree Nudleman gave no credence to the Tooth Fairy. She insisted the Tooth Fairy was as big a fib as Santa Claus, and told me I was a sucker for believing in grow-up garbage.

As my tongue teased my tooth, I watched Mikey's pudgy fingers pat the Jello in his bowl. "Lellow Jello!"

"Mikey," Mum reminded my little brother. "Jello is for eating, not for playing. Use the spoon."

"Poom. Poom." Mikey picked up his spoon, tapped his dessert, and stared, bug-eyed, as the golden globe wobbled. Mikey's Jello was like the sun rising out of the deep sky of its dish. He curled his chubby fingers around the glinting handle, dipped the oval end into the slippery orb, dropped a glob into his open, expectant beak, and cool sunlight slid down his throat. "Ahhhh." A beatific beam lit his full round face. "I like bazert!"

As my tooth twisted, I mused. If there really is a Tooth Fairy, he'd find my tooth no matter where I hid it. Mum and Daddy said the Tooth Fairy would fly in with a quarter. Mum and Daddy wouldn't lie to me.

The terminal tooth dropped onto my tongue. I removed it, like a wad of gum, and stuck it up my right nostril. As soon as I did, I had doubts. Maybe there really isn't a Tooth Fairy, after all – nobody I knew had seen one. And anyway, how would a Tooth Fairy know whose tooth had fallen out, and which pillow to visit? I grew uneasy. Teeth were supposed to sit inside mouths; they weren't meant to ride up noses. I attempted to retrieve my tooth, but it had already disappeared.

Mum was gulping coffee, and Daddy was nursing his nightly glass of tea. Maybe, I reflected, maybe it would be better to tell them.

"Abram! The car!" Mum erupted. She scooped Mikey into her arms and herded us onto the street and into the green Chevrolet. Only the front of the car had functioning doors. Deliberately. Mikey and I had been taught to climb into the back, and to stay there, so we couldn't fall out.

"But why?" Daddy turned from the steering wheel, to Mum. "Why did the child do such a thing?" Mum's gender, Daddy believed, gave her clairvoyant understanding of his children.

"With her imagination?" My creative imagination was a double-edged sword. "Who knows?!"

Daddy sped to the Jewish General Hospital.

"Sharon is sick?" Mikey was unnerved by the abrupt shift in environment. X-rays were taken of the inside of my nose, but nothing was found.

"Some kids will do anything for attention." The attending physician glared at me. "We have more important things to do." He cast a cursory glance at my frightened parents. "Relax," he growled. "Take her home."

"Sharon? Why did you make up such a story?" It wasn't an accusation. Mum knew it wasn't in my gentle nature to intentionally cause trouble.

"I didn't make it up."

"But the doctor says he can't find anything."

"I don't make up stories!" Generally a docile child, I now flared at the doctor. "I'm not a liar! I don't tell lies!"

We shuffled out of the hospital and into the car. I slumped sulkily in the back. Mikey patted my hand, in sympathy. No one believed me when I told the truth. Not ever.

Several days later, on Sunday, in the afternoon, Mum received a call from the hospital. An alert intern, struck by my staunch defence of personal integrity, re-examined the X-ray, and located the tooth.

I was taken from my family and led into a room that was bare except for a long table and a tray filled with sharp metal instruments. There were two nurses, and two interns. Dr. Inhaber had been located on a golf course. The four subordinates were waiting for him to arrive. I was told to take off my shoes and lie on the table. Inhaber entered, scowling. Some stupid kid had spoiled his game. Bypassing anaesthesia, the specialist raised forceps and rammed them up my nostril. I shrieked. Blood spurted out my nose like oil gushing from a well.

"Shut up." Inhaber barked. I gasped in shock. "I said shut up!" Inhaber smacked my rosy, tender cheeks. "I can't work like this." Inhaber turned to his impassive assistants. "Hold her down." The nurses rushed behind my head. One grabbed hold of my right wrist; the other grabbed my left. One intern pinned down my left ankle; the other bore down on my right. Inhaber, pacified, picked up the forceps again and thrust swiftly, deeply, repeatedly, penetrating high into my head. Fountains of blood spouted through my nose, drenching my dress and the doctor's lab coat. I wailed in agony. Inhaber struck me across the face. Blood flowed from my nares and stained the doctor's hands. "How many times do I have to tell you to belt up, brat!" My screams turned to sobs as Inhaber slid long metal daggers up my nose and into my head. My fists beat against the nurses, and my feet kicked against the interns. One of the young doctors, his wrists growing tired, sat on my turned-out ankle.

The pools of blood encircling my eyes blinded me. My sobs turned to gulps, and my whelps grew weaker. There was no mercy. I remained conscious.

On hearing my tortured howls, Mikey broke away from our parents and charged towards the source of the sound. He stretched up onto his toes, pushing at the doorknob of the examination room. It refused to turn. He pounded on the locked door. He hammered at the block of concrete and launched his stocky body against it like a battering ram.

"Shashi! Shashi!" Tears splashed his cherubic cheeks. "Dey killing my shister! Dey killing my shister!!!" He pleaded for help to the human traffic in the hospital corridor. He latched onto passing lab coats; he appealed to the humanity of nurses. "Help me! Please help me!" Our parents were sitting silently on a nearby bench. Mum held onto Daddy. Daddy's hands dangled between his knees. He hung his head like a miserable turtle.

"Do something, Daddy!" Mikey screamed, accusatory and confused. "Daddy! Why don't you do something?!" Daddy's limp hands flew to his anguished face. His hunched back convulsed. Mum held onto Daddy even harder, her slate blue eyes glazing over.

Unable to enlist assistance, Mikey hurled himself against the locked door. My cries had subsided to exhausted bleats. Mikey pinned his ear against the door.

"Shashi? Shashi?" Was I dead? "Open!" Mikey smashed his body against the door. It opened. Dr. Inhaber, his lab coat soaked in my blood, stepped out. Mikey leapt at him.

"I going to kill you!" He tackled the doctor's thigh and sunk his baby teeth into it.

Inhaber exploded. "Get this little monster off me!" Inhaber hopped on his free leg and tried to kick Mikey off his other one, but the tenacious toddler clung to the doctor's trousers, pressed his chest onto the doctor's knee, wept, clawed, grunted, bit and kept biting, as deeply and savagely as his strength allowed.

"I going to kill you," determinedly my little brother growled, between bites and tears. "I going to kill you!" Startlingly helpless, the specialist pleaded, "For heaven's sake, get him off me!"

Daddy raised his head. His moist chocolate eyes narrowed into dark slits. Mum dug her nails deeply into Daddy's arm. Daddy didn't move. Neither did Mum.

"What's the matter with you people?! Can't you see what he's doing? For crying out loud, I got the damn tooth! Now get this little monster off me!"

I limped out of the examination room. My head was swathed in blood-soaked bandages. Daddy rose to his feet. Slowly, he put one foot in front of the other. Even more slowly, he put the other foot in front of the one. At the pace of a drugged snail, he approached and pried his son off the doctor.

"It's alright, Mikey. Don't cry anymore. Shashi is alright."

"I going to kill him! Lemme at him!" Trapped in Daddy's arms, Mikey's limbs thrashed and flailed at the empty air. "I GOING TO KIIIIILL YOU!" Mikey howled down the hospital corridor. Dr. Inhaber escaped into an elevator.

Daddy relaxed his grip, and Mikey slid out of his arms. "Shashi?" He flew to me, and flung himself on me. "Oh Shashi!" Mikey squeezed me to him tighttighttight.

I no longer cried; my skull could not withstand the pressure of crying. Gently, I placed my aching arms on my brother's head, and stroked it. Mum took Mikey's hand, Daddy took my hand, and together we left the hospital, glumly trudging to the waiting Chevrolet which had only two functioning doors so that me and my little brother could sit safely in the back seats, without being in danger of falling out.

———————

WINTER, 2015

SETTING THE TEMPLATE

From the age of three, until I became eligible for kindergarten, I was enrolled at Mary Beetles in Montreal, a pre-school in the days before daycare programs, run by Miss Mary Beetles, a single and independent woman then referred to as a spinster, whose surname was spelled like the name of the insect, before a British pop group changed it.

On stage at a Christmas recital, I wore a pink dress with short puffed sleeves. A petticoat puffed up my short skirt, and a band of fake pink rose petals decorated my thick and dark hair. I was not yet self-conscious about my thick and heavy thighs, though I was acutely aware of the clunky, ankle-length orthopaedic shoes which encased my wide, flat and weak feet. I shook cymbals and tapped a tambourine. I had natural rhythm, effortlessly kept the beat, and felt perfectly comfortable on what was the first of many stages I would find myself on in years to come. The only light in the darkness of the hall emanated from the equipment of the hired photographer taking the pictures that were going to be sold to our parents once they were developed. The one disruption came from the back of the hall. A toddler seated on his mother's lap stretched for a better view of the stage, and suddenly erupted into a high-pitched scream.

"Dat's my shister! Dat's my shister!" He broke out of his mother's arms, dropped to the floor, tore up the centre aisle, and tried to hoist himself onto the stage.

Caught between footlights, with one chubby thigh on the boards, and straining to lift his diaper-covered bottom, my baby brother raised his luminous, blueberry-hued eyes, beaming his baby-toothed grin at me. "Shashi! Shashi!" Mikey called out the nickname he had given me. He seemed confused when I didn't dash over to help him, and surprised by the uncharacteristic scowl on my face. Clearly, he couldn't fathom why I wasn't as thrilled to see him as he was to see me.

Instinctively, I had grasped the concept and the convention of The Fourth Wall, and my adorable and adoring brother was breaking it! In this, my first crisis, I proved a trouper, stoically soldiering on while never missing a beat on my tambourine.

While the audience rocked with laughter, a policeman who had been standing guard at the back door rushed to the bottom of the stage, scooped Mikey into his arms, and carried him away.

"But she's my shister!" Mikey implored the policeman. Could the cop not comprehend the sacredness of the sibling bond? Oblivious to the giggles of the onlookers, patiently, pointedly, Mikey attempted to explain. "My SHISTER!"

The policeman merely smiled, and brought Mikey to the back of the hall.

Our recital proceeded without further incident. By the time it was over, the cop and the toddler had bonded. Mikey was leaning back, relaxed in the policeman's arms, with the policeman's oversized hat sliding down and masking the top half of his head.

Denied access to the main stage, the beguiling tyke created his own. While the cop held Mikey, Mikey's sweet and sunny nature held the cop enthralled.

In years to come, the world became my brother's stage. There were no barriers that could not be broken, no obstacles that could not be overcome, nor any arbitrary rules that could not be bent nor circumvented. Michael's irrepressible spirit and irresistible charm remain intact. So does his devotion to me.

WINTER, 2012

COMMUNIST HOT DOGS, IN PURSUIT OF PETULA, AND A KISS FROM MARLENE DIETRICH

The fiftieth anniversary of Expo '67 unleashes a flood of memories for me. As soon as season passes became available, passes which took the form of little red soft cover books with blank pages and were called "passports", my parents acquired "passports" for all four of us. These "passports" were stamped at the entry of each pavilion one visited. For six months in 1967, one could tour the world on two offshore islands adjacent to Montreal. When my little brother, who was eight at the time, had machine photos taken for his "passport", he grinned and crossed his eyes. Mischievously he insisted the cross-eyed picture was the one he wanted on his passport. My mother complied, but warned that each time he went through the gate he would have to cross his eyes or he wouldn't be recognized and the guards wouldn't let him in. Ultimately, she declared, his eyes would get stuck and stay crossed. Mikey would giggle. Then he'd cross his eyes again.

My parents were building a business and worked seven days a week, but on the Friday afternoon of April 27, 1967, they closed shop and, right after school, drove me and my little brother to St. Helen's Island and the new man-made island miraculously redeemed from the St. Lawrence River. At an inaugural ceremony 7,000 dignitaries were gathered, sixty-two national flags were unfurled, our prime minister lit the Expo torch, and we four family musketeers, along with a horde of Montreal's masses, charged through the opening gates.

The American pavilion and the Russian pavilion were poised at the edge of the two separate islands, confronting each other, connected by a small bridge that spanned the channel. Displaced by war, my dad spent five years as a refugee in Stalin's Soviet Union, a period which marked him for life. Dad wanted to see the Russian pavilion first. After touring the heavy-handed exhibition of tractors and spacecraft, for supper we went to the pavilion's cafeteria, where we had hot dogs wrapped in buns. All of us, even my little brother, smirked at the irony of eating typically American cuisine in the Russian pavilion. My parents were shocked at the price; seven dollars for four hot dogs in 1967! My father dubbed the meal "Goddam Communist hot dogs!" and nearly spat, "The difference between a capitalist and a communist is fifty bucks!" (Later, he would revise the "difference" to "100 bucks – because of inflation!") Nervously, my mother glanced at the Russian employees. In Polish, she hissed at her husband to behave himself.

"*Ach*! We're in Canada now! I can say whatever I want!"

My little brother nodded in solidarity. He glared at the sausage in his possession, just before chomping into it. "I am going to eat you, you communist!" With his mouth full, Mikey beamed beatifically at our dad. Daddy beamed back. Mikey adored our dad. So did I.

From then on we brought our own food. We spent weekends at the fair. Once word got out how marvellous it was, there were line-ups in front of the more popular pavilions that lasted for hours.

Less than a month later, during our brief time of lilacs, with the dandelion-studded grass a primavera green, the sky an unblemished blue, and the sun as yellow as in a child's crayon drawing, several classes in my elementary school were taken on a field trip to the Expo site. Our school was in a working-class neighbourhood and, for most of the children, this would be their only chance to experience the fair that the world's fortunate were flocking to see. Once we arrived at the site, our teacher did a head count and discovered one head missing. Norman, who was the fattest boy in class, just as I was the fattest girl, had managed to slip off the bus unnoticed. Eleven-year-old Norman had a crush on Petula Clark. He'd heard that the British pop singer had come all the way from "Downtown" to visit the Expo islands – so he waddled off in pursuit of Petula. The frightened teachers ordered our class to stay on the bus until Norman was found which, ultimately, took all afternoon. The bus door was locked, and we were imprisoned. The only technology then available for tracing a lost child in a crowd of thousands was a PA system. My classmates and I sat trapped, stewing in our seats until Norman was found. We never got off the bus. I knew that I would be able to come back, but the other kids had no such consolation. If I remember correctly, Norman was lured into an Expo office when a devious security guard paged Petula Clark. I cannot swear to it, but I think Norman got to meet his Pet, which must've made the punishment he received from his enraged classmates easier to bear.

Representing Canada, a family friend was employed as an Expo hostess during the Summer of Love. Anna was born in a displaced persons' camp in 1948, had a Teutonic surname, and spoke German before she spoke anything else. To her supervisors, this qualified the nineteen-year-old for the position of guide and factotum to Marlene Dietrich when the legendary star came to perform at the Expo Theatre. The sixty-seven-year-old icon warmed to Anna – in a motherly way. When Anna told her charge that her parents were coming to the evening's concert, Dietrich's impish side emerged. Onstage, she unexpectedly summoned the miniskirted hostess from the wings and introduced her to the audience. Then she pulled the pretty teenager to her and, with a lascivious look reminiscent of the cabaret scene in *Morocco*, Dietrich drew Anna into a cinema-style clinch and kissed her on the lips with grand, theatrical passion. The audience roared. Mama and Papa Bergmann, seated among them, swelled with pride and laughed as delightedly as the strangers in their midst. Anna's innocent parents never got the joke.

Having cleaned up my diet, I no longer eat hot dogs, but the sight of them recalls an obscure aspect of the Cold War. On the rare occasions when "Downtown" plays on the radio, I feel oddly claustrophobic. Dietrich's image in an old film makes me smile. Most of all, the memory of the education gained, the horizons expanded and the vision of a gleaming, glorious future incarnated on two magical islands for six months in 1967 will remain always.

AUTUMN, 2007

MY SECRET ADMIRER

It was summer, long ago. I was ten years old and at camp in southern Ontario. I hated volleyball and hiking because they made my flat feet hurt. I detested wearing shorts because they made my fat legs look fatter. I dreaded the overnight camping trips. How could I possibly "go in the bushes?" Luckily, we were always rained out and had to come back the same day.

The one spot I loved was the lake. I would wander off and sit on *my hamburger rock – I call it that because it looks like a giant hamburger* (I wrote in a letter I sent home), to watch sunbeams, like sequins, dance on the water, and contemplate the fireflies that flickered in the evenings under a velvet sky studded with stars as large as chunks of ice. I was artistic, unathletic, and my boredom with my bunkmates must've showed. They tormented me.

Ryan resided in the boys' bunk across from ours. He was my age. He would sit on the stoop, staring at no one, and nothing. He was tall, dark, skinny, and wore thick, black-framed glasses. He talked to no one; he played with no one. All summer he was perched on the porch of his bunk, like an owl. Little did I or anyone else realize that he was observing and absorbing – everything!

One day, an envelope was slipped under the door of my bunk addressed to "Miss Sharon". I grabbed the envelope before my bunkmates had a chance to tear it open. I took it down to my hamburger rock. When I was safely alone, I opened it. The letter was written with a cartridge pen in the "real writing" we'd all just learnt (as opposed to print), and it read: *Dear Miss Sharon.*

The other girls are mean to you because they're ignorant. They're jealous of you because you're better than they are. You are very intelligent, and you are very pretty.

You have very nice eyes, and very nice hair. Soon you will get braces, and when your teeth are fixed your smile will be even nicer. And don't worry, it's just baby fat. You'll grow out of it. When you're older, you'll get nicer glasses. Then when you grow up, you will be beautiful. Don't listen to those other girls. Don't let them hurt you. You will be fine. Everything will be OK.

It was signed, to my amazement (and this in big block letters). "YOUR FRIEND, RYAN".

I'd barely noticed Ryan, and when I did, like the others, I ignored him. I had a crush on Louis. Louis was an older man. He was sixteen, had blue eyes, blond hair, and didn't know I existed. Years later, I had occasion to speak to Louis. By then he was two inches shorter than me, and he was booooring.

The next afternoon I saw Ryan, as usual, chin in palm, sitting on the stoop. Shyly, I approached.

"Thank you very much for your letter, Ryan. It was really nice."

Ryan coughed, choked, mumbled, stuttered, and managed to splutter something like, "Zokay. You welcome."

I tried to talk to Ryan, but conversation was awkward and clumsy. He was more comfortable on the page, and it was in this intimate place that we conducted a private, enriching relationship in which we became each other's mutual secret admirers. This relationship was my introduction to a world I would come to inhabit as a working writer.

WINTER, 2004

OUR P.E.T.

It was early August, in 1968. My mother made me an offer. "You can have a month in camp, or spend a week at Stratford." For me, this was a no-brainer. I was twelve years old and obsessed with the theatre. I hated camp.

This was my first trip outside Quebec. My mother and I spent the week in Stratford attending Festival Theatre productions. We took a side trip to Niagara Falls, and then returned to Toronto to visit family friends. Now it was Friday, the end of our precious time together, and we were returning by train to Stratford for the evening performance of Chekhov's *The Seagull*, which was playing at the Avon Theatre.

Mum and I disembarked to find a crowd lining the depot of Stratford's tiny train station. We knew they weren't waiting for us, and actors in Stratford are as ubiquitous as squirrels in the park. "Maybe the Prime Minister is coming!" Mum trilled. But even Mum was startled when she turned out to be right.

It was the height of Trudeaumania, though not so much in Stratford, Ontario, which was conservative country. When we entered the Avon Theatre we saw Trudeau, Marchand and Pelletier, recently dubbed "The Three Wise Men", sitting in the centre of the ground floor flanked by plainclothes RCMP officers.

"Look at this!" Mum marvelled. "He isn't sitting in the front row, and he isn't sitting in a private box! Anyone could take a pot shot at him! He's a sitting duck for any crazy person. From where we are, I could shoot him right now! But here nobody does! Oh I'm so grateful the Americans didn't want me! What a wonderful country!"

My beautiful young mother, brimming with *joie de vivre*, was what the media would come to dub a Holocaust survivor. She adored her adopted country, which had belatedly opened its gates to refugees from war-torn Europe in 1948. She knew none of the words to *O Canada* except for the first two, and thought the lyrics, "our native land" referred to the Indians. But Mum would tear up whenever she saw the Canadian flag. No matter how tough their lot she would tell my dad, "Here in Canada, nobody's trying to kill us, we have the children, and we have each other." Particularly in 1968, after two political assassinations south of the border, Mum was grateful to have been transplanted to Canada.

At intermission, pen and theatre program in hand, Mum marched up as close as she could to the Prime Minister of Canada. Pierre Trudeau's political seat was in our Montreal riding, and Mum had proudly voted for him. A bodyguard stopped her. "I want to get his autograph!" Mum explained, stating her rights as a citizen. She was allowed to pass.

"Oh Mr. Trudeau! I live in your riding, in Montreal! I voted for you!" Flashing his famous grin, the Prime Minister graciously signed Mum's program.

"Oh Sharon!" she cried. "You should see! I got so close I could see his pockmarks!" As with Richard Burton, acne scars did not diminish Trudeau's appeal.

I was mildly interested in the Prime Minister's presence, but as a twelve-year-old I was more fascinated by a short and round young man I spied standing alone at the far end of the lobby. "Mummy look! It's Charlie Brown!" Only two months before in June, Mum and I had seen a Canadian touring production of *You're a Good Man, Charlie Brown,* when it made a pit stop in Montreal. The young man who played the lead was now in the lobby of the Avon, just a few feet away. "So it is!" Mum confirmed. "You wanna get his autograph?"

"Sure!"

Mum marched up to Charlie Brown while I tagged shyly behind. The young actor was surprised and delighted to be recognized. He was also mystified. "But Trudeau is here!" he protested. "Why would you be interested in me?"

For me, however, any actor was a demi-god. Knowing this, Mum took charge and soon she had Charlie Brown under her wing, as well as me. So it came to pass that me, Mum and Charlie Brown kept company in the lobby of the Avon Theatre on a sweet evening at the height of midsummer, when our new Prime Minister came to town to see a play.

Pierre Elliott Trudeau died on September 28. 2000 and, from then until the day of his funeral, Canadian society skidded to a halt. For five days, tributes and reminiscences poured into radio stations across the country. There were broadcasts of Trudeau's speeches. During that five-day period I finally heard and saw a bit of what my mother had experienced over thirty years before. Now, I was hearing them for what felt like the first time.

Breaking away from the broadcasts, I stepped into the streets of Montreal. Teen-age boys were razzing each other in English and French, switching languages so swiftly and deftly that one couldn't tell what their mother tongues were. There it was. Trudeau's legacy in action; bilingualism had become so firmly entrenched that it wasn't even an issue anymore.

On the streets I noticed predominately black, brown and yellow faces, and heard the sound of Spanish. This, I recognized, was the legacy of the open-door immigration policy initiated by Trudeau in the early 1970s. The acceptance of official bilingualism had paved the way for an acceptance of multiculturalism.

In Parliament, a political opponent laid a rose underneath Trudeau's portrait. In Montreal, at the entrance to Trudeau's mansion on Pine Avenue, political opponents as well as supporters laid roses at the foot of his door.

The train tracks along the Montreal-Ottawa route were lined with crowds of Canadians paying homage to their former and fallen leader. In Ottawa, Trudeau's body was taken to Parliament where he lay in state, and then returned to Montreal. It would be his last journey home.

In the wee hours of the morning Canadians stood by the railroad tracks, weeping. When the car bearing Trudeau's sons Justin and Sacha came into view, they spontaneously burst into cries of loving support, as well as applause.

In Montreal, the day of Trudeau's funeral was marked by the colour red; the red of the Canadian flag draped over his coffin, the red of the RCMP officers' jackets, the red of autumn leaves at their peak, and most of all, the velvety red of the roses being sold by street vendors and in florists' shops, and affixed to citizens' lapels. Trudeau was known for the red roses he routinely sported in the lapels of his dapper suits. On the day of his funeral, in early October, Montreal bloomed into a rose garden in honour and in memory of its beloved and lost P.E.T. – Pierre Elliot Trudeau.

WINTER, 2017

BLOOMING WHERE WE'RE PLANTED, AND A TASTE OF HONEY

We were a busload of older women off on a jaunt on a hot day in July. Departing from a Montreal seniors' center, we rode off to Mirabel, located in the Lower Laurentian Hills. In less than an hour we arrived at *Routes des Gerbes d'Angelica*, a collection of fourteen themed gardens which are the creation of twenty retirees who have invested their money and the rest of their lives, it seems, into creating and sustaining a sanctuary of natural beauty. Most of the money earned from this project (from parking fees and the food concession) is reinvested into this labour of love. The rest is donated to help support needy children, both here in Canada and in Indonesia.

The co-owners of this oasis have thought of everything; insect repellent is on hand in both spray and cream form. Large green (of course) parasols serve as added protection from the searing summer sun. As we passed through the gates of the various gardens, invisible sprinklers sprayed us with mist. In these dream gardens, it isn't only the flowers that are watered. Visitors are cooled off, too.

Our guides are women who won't see seventy again. Their bodies are tanned, fit and firm from work in the gardens. Their faces glow with the passion of spirits living life "on purpose". The work they're doing now with outlive them, and they know it. What a lovely gift they leave to posterity.

As we strolled languidly along garden paths, the scent of dahlias commingled with the humidity, distilling a singular tropic-like perfume.

"Why are the descriptions in French only?" A member of our group challenged the francophone guide.

"Originally we had bilingual descriptions, but the writing was of equal size. Someone complained, *et le gouvernment* told us we had to remove the English. (sic) We couldn't afford to redo the descriptions, making the French writing bigger." Quebec's latest language laws decree that French signs and typeface must be larger than corresponding English signs.

As we continued along the garden paths, I noticed one small bilingual descriptive plaque. It seems the language police are myopic.

At lunchtime I withdrew from the group huddled in the food concession under ceiling fans, and took myself to an outdoor table sheltered by an umbrella. There was one woman sitting at the table. She was not a member of our group. A video camera stood next to a chair. She was guarding it.

"May I sit here?" I asked, hoping to share the shade.

"*Mais bien sûr.*"

I laid out my lunch on the table. "Is that your camera?"

"It belongs to my husband. He'll be here soon."

On cue, the lady's husband arrived and took a seat. "Why are there no men in your group?" The man at the table noticed.

"They can't take the heat!" I riposted. "The only man with us is the chauffeur, and he's hiding on the air-conditioned bus!" That broke the ice, which would've melted in this weather, anyway.

My lunch companions were retirees who had come to take pictures and film of the gardens. "Usually we go to Ontario because the roads there are good, but we came here today because it isn't far." My lunch companions live in Pierrefonds, on the edge of Montreal's West Island.

The gentleman sitting opposite me began his professional life fifty years ago as a drummer with a rhythm and blues band. The band was known by various names, beginning with the moniker Iron Bag.

"It was serious fun! For five years we played all over and the others wanted to continue, but without a good manager to take us across Canada, we weren't going anywhere. Only one of us continues to make music. Dmitri. Jimmy. He is Greek. He makes music, but he doesn't make money." At this point, the gardener/guides surprised us with samplings of freeze-dried berries and cups of complimentary iced tea.

In 1975 my male lunch companion married Chantal, who was seated between us, and went to work for the federal government. They started a family and settled in Outremont. Thirty years ago they moved to The West Island.

"And what is your name?"

"I was Pierre, but I changed it, because the English called me Pee Uuurr. I will show you." The septuagenarian half-ran to the food concession, and returned with a brochure and a pen. On the brochure he proudly signed his autograph: PiAIRE. "So the English will know how to pronounce it!"

I smiled. "'Pierre' was good enough for Trudeau, but not for you?"

"You see! Pierre is banaaal! Everybody was Pierre!" Pierre/Piaire from Pierrefonds had a point. "But the Americans love Chantal!" Pierre/Piaire from Pierrefonds beamed at his bride of forty-four years. "They love to say 'Chantaaaal!' "

"For the Americans, *c'est exotique*. Do you go often to The States?"

"Well, I hate winter! We go to *Floride*. We go – Pierre/Piaire waved his hand as if he were sailing the high seas – *sur les croisieres."*

"Alors, votre pays n'est pas l'hiver." I was referring to the song that, for some, is Quebec's second national anthem. For some, *Mon Pays, C'est L'Hiver* is Quebec's only national anthem.

"*Non.*" Pierre/Piaire from Pierrefonds has taken his video camera around the world. His photographs and films are posted on YouTube. It appears that the federal government has been very good to Pierre/Piaire.

After lunch Pierre/Piaire picked up his camera and accompanied by Chantal, set off to film the gardens. Delicate flower that I am, I was wilting in the heat, so I climbed aboard a club car, alongside Nicole, one of the gardens' guardians who was serving as chauffeur. Nicole's sweet, mature face turned radiant as she pointed out the collective's creations. At the far end of the gardens there was a deer sanctuary, which fronted a vista of expansive meadows and rolling hills. The bus that brought us from Montreal stood at the edge of the meadows, shimmering in the heat.

On the way back to the *accueil*, under the protective roof of the club car, Nicole indicated a different kind of garden. Its archways led into a dark, shaded glade. Everyone still on their feet was heading for what seemed like a fairy-tale forest.

"Would you like to go inside?" Nicole was ready to stop the club car and let me off. I would've accepted her offer, but our bus was pulling up to the *accueil*. "The woods are lovely, dark and deep but…"

"It looks like we're going to leave."

"You must come back in winter. In winter this place is magic. There are thousands of lights strung up in the woods, and a fantasy village. Last year, during the week of Christmas, we had fifteen thousand visitors."

As our bus rolled out of Eden, Nicole and another guide stood by the side of the road, waving and shouting, "Come back! You must come back! Come back at Christmas!"

Fifteen minutes later we arrived at *Intermiel,* an internationally renowned honey farm founded by the Macles, two French teachers who came to Quebec fifty years ago. The Macles taught French on the West Island and raised a family while investing in their passion for beekeeping. Three years ago the Macles were able to fully devote themselves to their farm. Today *Intermiel* houses ten thousand beehives, and welcomes even more that amount of visitors annually.

Madame Macle greeted us, and then passed us on to a young beekeeper and guide. We watched a brief film of *Intermiel's* history, and then we were led to a screened-in porch, where we witnessed a demonstration of honey-in-the-making. Our young guide regaled us with an entertaining lecture on the sex lives of bees, before donning an astronaut-like white coat and helmet with a facial screen.

"They do their wiggle dance and then rub together their antennas. The rubbing sets off an electric charge. That's what gets the throat going. Honey is produced in the throat, but propolis is produced in the belly!" Oddly, the young beekeeper did not protect her hands before approaching a tray full of bees. When asked why not, she responded, "My bees know that if they bite they will die, so they don't bite unless they feel in danger." I still haven't wrapped my brain around that one.

When the beekeeper was asked, "What is the difference between a wasp and a bee?" I muttered to myself, but not completely to myself, "The bee wears a *yarmulke*." Fortunately, no one heard me.

The beekeeper smoked the bees out of hiding. Literally. She set off smoke, and the bees emerged from their hive. We were introduced to the queen bee. The queen bee seemed to resent this intrusion upon her privacy, and refused to grant us an audience. Defying her keeper, the royal insect flew back to the hive. I took this rebuff personally until the beekeeper, peering closely, burst, "Look! There is a new and younger queen bee! How can this be? This situation cannot be supported!" In beehives, as in human families, there can be only one queen.

The beekeeper was asked what would happen between the two queens. "One of them will be removed." She didn't say how. But from bitter experience, I knew. It is not only bees who sting. It is the older queen who will be forced to abdicate. What becomes of an ousted queen? If she is to survive, she goes into hiding. In order to escape the dangers of isolation then, wisely, she joins a seniors' center.

After this demonstration of rivalry and power, as well as the manufacturing of propolis, royal jelly, beeswax and honey (A teaspoon of honey represents the lifespan of one worker bee. Something to consider the next time one sweetens one's tea) we were directed to the souvenir shop. Scattered through the shop and the lobby were low chairs and benches strewn with cushions that read Bee Happy.

I eschewed the shop's thirty-dollar candles and ten-dollar bars of soap, but succumbed to a thirteen-dollar bottle of *Rosé* steeped in rose petals plucked from roses grown on the grounds. Madame Macle joined her cashiers and personally handled my purchase.

"Keep it in the refrigerator. An hour before serving, chill it in the freezer. When you open it, you can also add more rose petals."

Mais bien sûr.

Clutching our purses and purchases, our group of forty older women boarded the bus taking us back to Montreal. A fellow passenger had purchased a bottle of mead "because my sons are obsessed with the Middle Ages". I had a flash of Richard Burton and Peter O'Toole in period costume. Also Robin Hood.

We rode off the grounds of the honey farm in the heat of high summer. We had done a good job. We had contributed generously to the economy of Quebec.

———————

SUMMER, 2019

REMOVING SOCIAL MASKS

I went to the little fruit and veggie place on Cote St. Luc Road. *Soleil*, it's called. Its run by a toothless old Turk, his son Ely, and a black helper named Albert. I discovered this place before winter. It's a hole in the wall in the middle of nowhere, but the produce has always been of superior quality, and the atmosphere was friendly.

When I arrived there was a line-up in front of the door. A short one. Because the place is so small, now only two customers are allowed in, at a time.

I came up Cote St. Luc Road wheeling my trolley. Because of the pain in my leg, I was walking more slowly than usual. Because I had to wheel the trolley, I didn't carry a cane.

A young, petite, dark-haired woman wearing a mouth mask got out of a solid-looking white car parked in front of the store, and scooted in front of me.

"Looks like a tie." I said. She gave me a hard stare. She had pretty dark eyes. The mask covered the rest of her face. "Beauty before Age." She ignored my hint, and planted herself in front of me, at a distance.

While waiting, this woman got on her cell phone. From the inflection and quality of both her French and English, it was clear to me that she was a Moroccan Jewess.

The Masked Moroccan went into the store ahead of me, but my turn came soon, so we were in the store at the same time. Quietly I selected my items. I noticed that, since this lockdown, the quality of the produce has deteriorated. It was obvious that The Masked Moroccan was a regular customer. At the very least she was a valued customer and, it would turn out, also a valuable one.

Ely, the youngish son of the toothless Turk, began a conversation with The Masked Moroccan. It may not have been a flirtation, but it was a dance. Ely began the conversation by saying, "My brother is now on the Covid ward." I was startled. To The Masked Moroccan he clarified. The grocer's brother is a doctor, working in a private hospital in Turkey. "He was offered a position here, but he can make a lot more money there, and the weather can't be beat." Is that the reason why one becomes a doctor? It seemed Ely knew that The Masked Moroccan is a medical person. Supposedly she is a nurse who now is working from home. (How does a nurse work from home?) Her husband is a cancer surgeon at the Jewish General Hospital.

Listening to this conversation distracted me and slowed me down. The impression I got was that the grocer was trying to impress the wife of a doctor that he, too, was related to a doctor. Talking slowed down The Masked Moroccan even more than it slowed me down and, it turned out, she had a lot more shopping to do than I did, because she was shopping not only for her immediate family, which includes children, but also for her mother and aunt.

While The Masked Moroccan took her time with shopping and conversation, the queue outside the door lengthened. An angry voice was raised and pierced the closed doors. "What's going on in there?! When are we going to get in!" From behind the counter, at the cash, the Toothless Turk sprang into action. He turned on ME. "Hurry up!" I headed to the cash, but once more The Masked Moroccan sprung in front of me. "We're all in the same boat," serenely, she pronounced. Once more, I had to wait behind her. The Masked Moroccan's order was massive. My wait was long, but my order was processed quickly. When I wheeled my loaded trolley down the steps and came outside I saw that a very long queue had formed. Several people in the line were blacks. Poor blacks. The Masked Moroccan swanned onto the street, her arms empty, while the black helper Albert lugged what appeared to be a dozen bags to her snow-white car.

"Discrimination!" A black man, or woman, screamed from the middle of the queue. (Hard to tell, under the mouth masks) "It's discrimination!" Oblivious, The Masked Moroccan glided into her car and sailed away. It was the young grocer who had to deal with the fall-out, and he did. Ely leapt onto the steps that led to the little store and planted himself firmly in front of what was developing into an angry mob.

"Discrimination?!" He bellowed, as Black Albert hid in the shop. "You know me?! Do I do discrimination?!" (I don't know. Do you do windows?) "In my neighbourhood I had to wait two hours before getting into IGA! If you don't want to wait, you can go!" The skinny, skin-headed grocer with fierce dark eyes trembled. He was genuinely unconscious of the part he played in creating this scene by favouring one wealthy, self-centred customer over a line of others. "Nobody gives me a hard time!"

There was grumbling among the masses. I decided to hightail it down Cote St. Luc Road before a race riot broke out.

I wasn't in the same boat as The Masked Moroccan. I wasn't even in the same car. I had to wait for a bus to take me back to my side of the neighbourhood. When I got home I exchanged my trolley for a cane and went back outside to walk. Then I sat silently in the library garden. I remained in silence for the rest of the day. So this is it, I thought. This is the way it's going to be for the foreseeable future, and a foreseeable future is all I've got. I'll never travel overseas, again. I'll never see more of the world, before leaving it. All I'm going to get is trips to grocery stores, where I'll witness scenes such as this one.

―――――――――

SPRING, 2020

THE WONDERFUL WORLD OF TRAVEL

A Tale of the Pandemic

Through a neighbourhood travel agent, in December 2019 I booked a tour of northern Italy, scheduled for May 2020. I also bought an expensive and comprehensive insurance policy which would allow me to cancel FOR ANY REASON. I stumbled upon this agent's office in a local mall during the late winter of 2019. I told her that I was alone and on a limited budget. She told me there was a tour company that catered for solo travellers, and ordered their brochure for me in advance of the 2020 season.

The agent booked my ticket through a wholesaler. When I asked to reserve a window seat I was told I had to pay for reserved seating. This surprised me, but since I hadn't been on an overseas flight in twenty years I accepted it. After all, I was dealing with a licensed agent who had been in business for twenty-five years.

In February the agent notified me that I had been bumped from a scheduled flight and was being transferred onto another one. When I asked what would happen to the reserved seat for which I paid extra her response was, "What difference does it make? You'll make your connecting flight."

On Sunday, March 1, the American Center for Disease Control issued a travel advisory on northern Italy. The same day, Delta Airlines cancelled all its New York-Milan flights until May 1. I was scheduled to fly from New York to Milan. My flight was scheduled for May 5, so it wasn't cancelled – yet.

On Monday, March 2, the Canadian government issued a travel advisory on northern Italy. On Thursday, March 5, the tour company cancelled the Italian Lakes tour. When the tour was cancelled, I asked the travel agent to cancel my flight. Though she had sold me an expensive Cancellation For Any Reason policy, she refused to do so. She urged me to wait for Delta to cancel my flight. "This way we won't have to go through insurance. If Delta cancels, you'll automatically receive a refund. It will be a lot easier, this way. I know my business. Trust me. I've got you covered."

In the ensuing weeks, a new law was created stating that anyone who purchased an airline ticket before January 21, 2020 (on January 20, WHO officially recognized the virus as a global threat) was automatically entitled to a full refund, whether they had purchased insurance, or not. I had.

On Wednesday, April 15, Delta cancelled my flight. Which is when, after e-mailing the notice from Delta, the travel agent called and instructed; "Now you pay a processing fee."

"What processing fee? I don't understand. You said if the airline cancels, then I don't have to pay any fees. You said there would be a fifty-dollar fee if I cancelled, but if Delta cancels I would receive a refund automatically. Isn't that why we waited?"

For me, while witnessing Italy's agony, the five weeks between the cancellation of the tour and the cancellation of the flight was a nerve-wracking wait. Many people went through this "wait", but I didn't have to. I had complete and comprehensive coverage.

On the phone line there was an almost imperceptible hesitation. Less than a pause, more than a beat. Then the travel agent responded, almost too quickly, "You misunderstood. If you had cancelled, Delta's fee would've been much more than fifty dollars. But because THEY cancelled it's ONLY fifty dollars. Actually fifty-two, with the tax. It's the flight that's cancelled, not your ticket. If you don't pay the processing fee then the airline won't cancel your ticket. Instead, you'll get credit. And Delta could go bankrupt. But don't worry. You'll get the money back on the fee. We'll claim it from insurance."

I accepted, and hung up. Then I remembered that my credit card was reaching its expiry date, and I had activated a new one. I called the travel agent to give her my new credit card number so she could charge Delta's "processing fee" to my card.

On Saturday, April 18, I received another call from the travel agent bearing "Good news!" This news was so good that instead of e-mailing, once more, the travel agent called. And on the weekend, too. I was told that if I paid Delta's "fee" out of pocket (which was, I began to suspect and would later have confirmed, a fee invented by the imaginative travel agent), along with a thirty per cent "penalty" (which would also prove a work of fiction by the creative travel agent) to Manulife, (the insurance company), then Manulife would refund seventy per cent of the price of the insurance policy.

"But why would I give up my insurance? It's – it's – insurance! It's meant to protect me! Especially with what's going on now! You said Delta might go bankrupt! What if I don't get my refund? Then at least I'm covered by insurance."

"You'll get your refund. I issued it on Wednesday. Even if Delta goes bankrupt you'll get your refund because once the refund has been issued the money is out of Delta's hands. It's gone to Visa. Delta can't retrieve it. YOUR REFUND HAS BEEN PROCESSED. Whatever happens to Delta, you'll get your refund. Expect to see it in three months. And even if you didn't get your refund from Delta, I've got insurance. You're protected because instead of booking the trip on your own, you went through a licensed travel agent. I wouldn't propose this to you unless I was sure that your refund is safe." Then the travel agent's soothing tone turned harsh, and the bullying began. "Don't you know the difference between 52 dollars and 197?!" Fifty-two dollars was the amount of Delta's supposed fee, and 197 is what would be left after I paid Manulife a 30 percent penalty. My refund was becoming expensive.

"I know the difference between 127 dollars and fourteen hundred!" Which was the price of my ticket, the taxes, and the reserved seat.

I don't consider myself a stupid person, or a particularly weak one, but the travel agent had all the answers before I asked the questions, and I finally succumbed.

"O.K. So have Manulife deduct their 30 percent penalty, and send me the rest."

"It doesn't work that way." The travel agent's tone turned confidential. "I've got a friend who works there. She expects to lose her job in the next few weeks. She told me privately that Manulife is going bankrupt." (Another major institution going bankrupt? At the height of the first lockdown, everything seemed possible.) "But she says she'll help us out. I have to pay her privately so she'll issue the 70 per cent refund. Which means you have to pay me directly so that I can pay her. You make out a cheque to me. This is a good deal. I urge you to take it. If not, you'll lose everything."

"Fine, I can bring you a cheque on Monday."

"Monday may be too late. Manulife could be bankrupt by Monday. My office is closed, so you can come to my home." (Which is in the neighbourhood.)

Caught in the force of momentum, on Sunday afternoon, April 19, in torrential rain, with an umbrella in one hand and a cane in the other (I don't have a car. I can't afford one), I limped to the travel agent's large family home. With a great grin, she greeted me from behind a wide front window. She opened her door a crack and snatched the cheque from my hand. Then she slammed the door in my face.

I didn't sleep that night. I felt awful. What had I done? How gullible could I be?

At 9 am on Monday, April 20, I called Manulife. My call was transferred to their travel department.

"Why are you willing to refund part of what I paid for the travel insurance policy? Why are you being so generous?"

"What?! But we issued a full refund to you on Friday! It's already in process! We don't usually do that, but the travel agent convinced us to do it because there was no claim."

"Not even a claim for fifty two dollars?"

"No. Nothing. No claim. We've sent you a full refund. 275.73. Don't you want it?"

No wonder the travel agent twisted my arm. Having succeeded in scamming me once, she was so sure she'd be able to extort more money from me that she cancelled my travel insurance even before we spoke. She was almost right.

My next call was to my bank. "We can stop the cheque now, but if it's already gone through, there's nothing we can do."

I wrote the cheque on Sunday the 19th, but dated it for Monday, the 20th. It was just before 9:30 on Monday morning. I am a generation older than the travel agent. I did not realize that she had already deposited the cheque through her phone. Still, the cheque was successfully arrested because, I assume, we dealt with different banks, and there is a two-day hold on transactions from one bank to another.

I notified the travel agent that I had stopped the cheque. She was furious. "But I've already deposited it! If I deposit a stopped cheque the bank will charge me a fifty-dollar penalty! I'm not going to pay fifty dollars! If that cheque doesn't go through and I'm stuck with a penalty, YOU'RE going to pay it!"

The cheque did not go through. I do not know if the travel agent was charged a penalty, because she never told me. What she did was to call and wheedle, "I'll give you another chance. Come on. Write me another cheque. It'll be the last one. After this, you won't have to pay any more." Then she offered an alternative. "If you don't want to write me a cheque, you can bring me cash."

I declined the travel agent's latest offer. Instead, I called Delta. Checking the date and time of the cancelled flight against the credit card number under which it was issued; I was told that I would receive my refund "between three weeks and a month".

"Really? That soon? I was told three months."

Testily the Delta agent repeated, "Between three weeks and one month."

My next call was to Visa. "I want to stop my card, but I have a refund coming through. What will happen if I stop the card before receiving the refund?"

"The refund will be transferred onto the new card. But why do you want to stop your card?"

"To prevent fraud." I told my story to the Visa rep. I assume she was a young woman. She had a young voice.

"Something similar happened to my grandmother!" The Visa rep erupted. "She hasn't travelled for a long time and she went to a travel agent to help her book a trip. When the flight was cancelled the agent started bullying her and wouldn't give her a refund. Just because my grandmother is an older woman, it doesn't mean she can be pushed around! We work, we're busy, but we care! I went to the travel agent with my grandmother and you better believe she changed her tune!"

"It stinks, doesn't it?" I interjected. "Doctors have died trying to save lives, and travel agents exploit a global tragedy."

"My grandmother isn't alone and nobody is going to think so!" The Visa rep was almost crying. "I'm not going to let anybody push around my grandmother!"

My credit card was stopped.

A month later, I still hadn't received the refund. Once more, I called Delta. This time, I was transferred to the refund department. After forty-five minutes on hold, I reached them.

I was never going to receive the refund. It was never issued. The Delta agent exploded. "Your travel agent dropped the ball!"

I told the Delta agent my story. Like the Visa rep, he erupted. "You bought an airline ticket, not a gift card. If you had cancelled then yes, there would have been fees. But we cancelled, so there are no fees. If your travel agent extorted a fee from you in our name then she committed fraud. She also made us look bad. I'm sorry you've been put through this. I hope you'll come back to Delta."

"Well, if I can get my money back then I'll be able to reinvest it when the time is right. But I'm not rolling in dough. It took me years to save for this trip and I don't have that many years left. I can't afford to lose money."

"Under normal circumstances, you'd receive your refund within a month. But we're swamped. Right now we're working on refunds for flights that were scheduled to fly in late March. We'll examine this."

"I understand."

"Unfortunately, there's another layer. Because of the way the travel agent issued your ticket, we can't send you a refund. She issued it through a wholesaler, so if we were to issue a refund, we'd be obligated to send it there. The wholesaler would be obligated to forward the refund to you."

"Wasn't the travel agent obligated to send my refund to me?"

To this, the Delta rep had no reply. I told him how much I paid for the ticket. Slowly and carefully, he responded, "I can't see how much is owed to you. The agent may have padded your bill. Because of the way the agent issued the ticket, the information is blacked out. I can't even see who the wholesaler is. She cut us out of the loop."

And I no longer had insurance.

On Tuesday morning, August 11, I was lying on the grass outside the deck of the outdoor community pool. I listened to voices coming from the water. One voice stood out. It was the loudest mouth in the pool. It was the voice of the travel agent.

On this hot summer morning, many people were at and in the water. Almost every recreational facility is closed and no one is traveling. Not even a travel agent.

I lay on the grass, and thought about it. Then I got up, went to another section of the large pool, dunked, cooled off, and thought about it. Then I threw on my sundress, packed my gear, and thought about it. Then I stood and approached the pool deck.

"Mrs. Cohen," I called, "when can I expect my refund!"

The travel agent was surrounded by a bevy of admirers. She is a local *vedette*. Everyone knows her.

Ruth Cohen was quick on the draw. From the water she shouted, to the sky, to the crowd, and to me, "You're not gonna get it 'cause YOU'RE A BITCH!

On the pool deck, I stood my ground. "Regardless. I am still legally entitled to a refund."

"Take it outside!" Another woman in the water shouted at me. It was to be expected. I was making a fuss. I was making a scene. Even worse, I was being unpleasant.

"No." I cut off the woman in the water. "I want witnesses."

Ruth Cohen blinked. Her voice seemed to weaken. "You can't get a refund because Delta is only giving credit."

I glared at her. "I called Delta." In the water, Ruth Cohen appeared to gulp, like a guppy. I repeated, almost shouting. "I called Delta!" Ruth Cohen shut up. At least, she shut up to me. As I was leaving I noticed a group of curious onlookers in the water surround her, like an ambush.

"What happened? Who is she?!"

Caught, Ruth Cohen blustered, "She's abnormal! She's abnormal! She's just abnormal!"

I went home. While Ruth Cohen was holding court in the sunshine, I was lying alone in a darkened room, gasping for breath and feeling something I've never felt before. The pressure was prolonged and severe. I sent a message to my brother, who is a physician in Ontario. The instant he received it, he called.

"At our age," my slightly younger brother intoned in the doctor's voice he dons when an alarm goes off, "chest pains are serious."

Your money, or your life?

───────

AUTUMN, 2020

LET THE GOOD TIMES ROLL

In the middle of the month I attended a rock 'n' roll concert in a local park. After three years of restrictions, it was a pleasure to mingle with people who were fully enjoying themselves. What was wonderful was the air. It was fresh. Almost soft, the way air should feel on a summer evening. The sky was blue, with white clouds in it. There was a breeze. After weeks of wildfires and heatwaves, on the eve of a near-tornado, this evening's air felt like the whiff of an old perfume.

The band performing was called Vintage Wine. This band has been coming to my neighbourhood every summer for years. The baby of the band was forty-four years old. The other band members were in their sixties, and even in their seventies. At one point they belted out The Stones' *I Can't Get No Satisfaction,* though they didn't dare attempt Rod Stewart's *Do Ya Think I'm Sexy.*

The majority of the audience was of the same generation. So were the neighbourhood V cops (volunteer cops) who, on this evening in the park, were mostly female. Identifiable by their bright orange and yellow vests, they bopped along the park paths in time to the music. One grey-haired little V Cop erupted into a full-blown dance. And she was good! There were couples rockin' and rollin'. Women on their own shimmied with each other. During a 1950s slow number, an elderly couple entwined and swayed in a locked embrace. Those who came by car – the park's parking lot was full, and cars lined the streets, too – brought and set up canvas chairs. I stood under and against a tree bathed in a setting sun. When I got tired of standing – and bopping – I headed further into the park and sat on a bench in front of fountains, watching children frolic and splash among the spouts. People smiled at each other, and a few smiled at me. When I returned to a spot close to the bandstand, one of the V cops engaged me in conversation. "You look like you're enjoying yourself." She noticed. What a pre-pandemic thing to say and do.

One young woman was filming the concert with her phone. I don't understand this. One can find everything on YouTube these days, so why not just show up and enjoy the moment? Another young woman asked a V cop for directions to the bar. There was no bar. "But it's called Vintage Wine!"

At the end of the concert the local mayor and his wife glided up a path like a pair of swans. They deigned to the crowd as though they were Charles and Camilla.

All in all, a good time was had by all. May there be more to come.

SUMMER, 2023

THE SOUNDTRACK OF OUR LIVES

They were four lads from Liverpool. Born in war and raised in austerity, they formed a band of musical brothers that made Britain swing and Europe smile. They were vital, tenderly young, and having the time of their lives. They conquered America less than three months after the first Kennedy assassination. For Ringo, The Endearing One, and the eldest, the best part of their first overseas tour was "All of it! Especially Miami, because of the sun!" For John, The Intelligent One, and the cheekiest, America's music and social mobility proved siren calls luring him to an early and violent death.

It was George, The Quiet One, and the youngest, who was most conscious of the peril provoked by their spectacular fame. In 1964, he refused to participate in a ticker tape parade held in San Francisco. Yet the first serious threat would come, not from the recently traumatized Americans, but from a cosy northern corner of this continent. It was at the beginning of the school year in September, 1964, that The Beatles were scheduled to perform at the Forum in Montreal. Of course I wanted to attend the concert. Since I was only eight years old I expected my dad to not only buy me a ticket, but to purchase a second ticket and come with me. It was one of the few times in our time together that my father said No. It was not a regretful refusal; it was a vehement one. He envisioned and vociferously described how we would be trampled and crushed into powder by a horde of hysterical adolescents if we dared to go. What my dad could not know; what the general public did not know for decades to come is that the xenophobic hate mongers who stain Quebec were not about to tolerate another British invasion. At that time there were cells of Separatist thugs who had a bad habit of placing bombs in mailboxes, instead of letters. These hoodlums had decided that the blissful, bopping Ringo was not only

English, but also Jewish, and for these twin crimes, they were going to kill him. That Ringo was English was obvious and irrefutable. That Ringo was Jewish was untrue and to racists, irrelevant. He had a protruding nose, wore large, flashy rings, and had transformed his original surname of Starkey into the stage name of Starr. An official death threat was issued, and Montreal police responded in their usual manner. On the night of the concert, they sent a plainclothes policeman to sit on the riser with Ringo. Ringo raised the cymbals on his drum kit, hoping they might afford him an iota of protection. As the concert progressed Ringo would glance at the cop, wondering what he might do in case of an attack. He soon realized that what would be done was nothing. Because The Beatles, unlike their audience, were neither accustomed nor resigned to ineffectual cops. They left Montreal the next day, never to return, as a group, again.

In December of 1980, I was traveling through northern Greece. It would be the week before Christmas, upon my return to Athens, when I stumbled upon a ten-day-old issue of *Time* Magazine. A discontented working-class lout, rescued through music, had walked into a fatal confrontation with his Shadow Side. John's murder sent a generation into mourning for its lost innocence. I felt so far away from home.

The three remaining Beatles came together over John, and then went their separate ways. Simple Ringo, whose greatest ambition had been to own a chain of hair salons, floundered and lost his footing before reclaiming sobriety and settling into a contented second marriage with a former Bond Girl.

Paul, The Cute One, always a charmer, appeared to be leading a charmed life. He was lauded, feted, and ultimately knighted. The last to marry, his first marriage, unlike those of the other three, would've been his last had not breast cancer claimed his Linda, as it had taken his mother over forty years before.

It was George's post-Beatle existence which appeared the most fulfilling, until he was waylaid by the cancer and the violence that have been added to the soundtrack of our lives. When madness descended upon George it came in the proverbial peaceful English countryside. An intruder found his way onto George's secluded estate. He believed God had sent him on a mission to kill The Quiet Beatle, and his mission almost succeeded. Having survived throat cancer, George now sustained forty stab wounds, including wounds to a lung, which punctured it, before his wife subdued the assailant by bludgeoning him with a fireplace poker and a lamp.

George's cancer returned, spreading from his lungs to his brain. As the ex-Beatle lay dying the attending doctor insisted upon an autograph. George protested that he could barely remember his name, let alone write it, so the accommodating doctor forced his hand.

The two Beatles destined to reach old age came together over George. Ringo had to leave earlier than intended in order to fly to his daughter, who was undergoing brain surgery. George perked up, and the quirky British wit we fell in love with when we were young and uncompromised, bubbled to the surface one final time. "Would you like me to come with you?" he quipped, to his departing friend.

George joined John. The two surviving Beatles got older. We got older. Life got hard. We aren't carefree anymore.

WINTER, 2013

ERIC'S SECRET

or

READER: I DIDN'T MARRY HIM

On the morning of June 27, 2015 I woke too early, with a start, thinking of a man I hadn't spoken to in decades and haven't seen in years. His memory pressed in upon me. I grew agitated. I opened the computer and consulted my assistant Google. Quickly I found what, subconsciously, I was looking for; the obituary of Eric P. He died on either June 16 or June 17, depending on whether one consulted the synagogue obituary or the funeral parlour's website, and his *shiva,* held in a predominantly Jewish Montreal suburb, had ended less than forty-eight hours before. For most of the day I resisted the idea that Eric's spirit had contacted me. For the past two decades, while Eric was embodied, he would bolt whenever he saw me, taking off so fast that he left skid marks. Did he now feel free to reach out because he had left society behind? It felt that way. Still, I had a hard time believing it. *If you're contacting me from The Other Side then send me another sign.* Silently, I beseeched his spirit. Within hours, I received the requested sign.

Eric's timing seemed typical of him. It was slightly off, without being completely off. He may have wanted me to know that he has been removed, but he waited until the earthly rituals were over so that I wouldn't be tempted to attend them. He was self-protective and self-centred beyond the end. I would not have been tempted to attend Eric's funeral, and I would never have gone near what I now realize must be the home of one of his children.

It was only once before that I looked up Eric P on the Internet. It was a year before, in the depths of bereavement.

What I found was a video of Eric skiing in his ninetieth year. My mother was younger than Eric, and she had recently died, but Eric was still out there, and he was still skiing. What I felt was bitter and resentful that Eric outlived my mother. It was my mother who became the love of my life.

I met Eric P in the late 1980s, at an institute for adult education. He was one of three facilitators in a course I took. I was attracted to this silver-haired gentleman almost from the moment I walked into the room. He was elegant, cultured, sophisticated and poised. He had a slight inflection in his tenor voice which I believed I recognized. I approached him after the class and blurted, "Are you a Polish Jew?" Eric smiled ironically. "I used to be."

Eric P was born in Łódź eight years earlier than he would lead me to believe. He was an offshoot of a lesser branch of the family of industrialists immortalized in I.J. Singer's *The Brothers Ashkenazi*. This piece of information impressed my mother. Eric was also a distant cousin of Alicia Posnanska Parizeau, the recently deceased wife of the Quebec premiere who was threatening to destroy Canada. This piece of information left my mother indifferent.

Eric went to England to study in late August of 1939 and sensibly, never turned back. I don't know how he was brought to Canada, but after extricating myself from his influence I would later learn that he married in 1945 to a very Canadian Jew. The same source told me that they were young sweethearts, and the one bone of contention in their marriage was that Eric wanted to wait until they were older before being saddled with children, and Ruth didn't. Ruth got her way. By the time Eric died, at the age of ninety-three, he was a great-grandfather.

In the class at the Thomas More Institute my intelligent questions, my youth, and my background soon caught Eric's attention. I was a young Jewish woman from a family of Holocaust survivors in an institute for adult learning comprised of blue-eyed, white-haired WASPs. (Whenever I find myself in a room full of Gentiles, I tend to get into trouble with the other Jew.)

After class, Eric began offering lifts to my downtown apartment, and I accepted them. He would sound me out, but say little about himself. He would speak about his pre-war background but, except for letting me know when he would be away on business trips, Eric maintained a veil of secrecy over his present-day life.

In order to extend our private time Eric would drive us up to Summit Circle, where we would go for walks. He lived in Westmount, at the top of the hill and the social scale, and during these late evening walks he told me stories about the people who lived in the mansions on Summit. I believe he looked forward to our after-class drives as much as I did. Looking back on that spring, I believe Eric went through several phases of feelings for me. It began with curiosity. It progressed to contemplating if he could safely indulge in a sexual fling. Eric was clever and careful, and he wasn't a brute. Accurately he perceived that he was dealing with an extremely sensitive and vulnerable young woman who would be shattered by a casual affair. I don't doubt that when Eric was young he indulged in discreet dalliances on business trips, but getting involved with a sweet and intense Jewish woman from Cote St. Luc who had recently lost her father was too close for comfort. Eric was not only the father of daughters; he was also a grandfather. I believe the qualities in me that caused Eric to step on the brakes also touched his heart. By the time the course ended in late June I was in love, and Eric was in – something. We had known each other for several months, and in all that time he never mentioned a wife or children. I didn't dare ask. I was afraid of the answer. I was hoping against hope that he was either divorced or widowed. I was also hoping he'd simply come clean, and tell me.

After the last class, after seeing me to my door, Eric dropped the charm, dispensed with flirtation, gripped my hands in his and implored, "How can I see you again?" Not when, but how. Eric's hands were as naked as mine. He wasn't wearing a wedding ring.

I was stunned. I could barely breathe. All spring I felt as though I'd been reaching for the moon. Now, it seemed the moon was reaching for me.

"I'm a phone call away." I was amazed at my logic and calm.

Eric did not call. I didn't expect him to. Sadly I decided that I would not return to Thomas More in the autumn.

In late September, accompanying my mother, I attended the premiere of the Polish film *Korczak*. I was temporarily living with my mother. I had broken the lease on my downtown apartment and had to wait three months before my next apartment became available. Eric was at the premiere, attending with a Polish friend who was an acquaintance of my mother's. When he saw me, his eyes lit up. The two men approached. I stood tongue-tied. My mother leapt in and did the talking for me. Mum could be as charming as Eric. At the end of the evening, safe in a social circle, Eric introduced me to his wife.

"That guy's really got a crush on you," my mother confirmed. "He circles you like an infatuated schoolboy."

"The feeling is mutual," I confessed.

"Well, if it were any other old guy I'd say you're nuts, but in this case I understand the attraction. Too bad he isn't twenty years younger and available. Maybe he has a son?"

"Oh Ma."

"So, are you going back to class?"

"Yes," I confessed again, like a condemned man stepping up to the gallows.

"Oh kiddo," my mother couldn't stop me, and she knew it. "You're a masochist."

Going back for the autumn semester of 1990 meant travelling downtown by public transportation from my mother's suburban apartment. I did so on the understanding that Eric would be going well out of his way in order to drive me home. In this, at least, I was not disappointed. There was a new tone to our exchanges, both in the classroom and in the car. Eric was relaxed. I was resigned. Eric set the tone for a platonic love affair conducted within severely restricted limits. He would tell me about his children, but not about his wife. He would speak love to me in code, the way he would later speak of his love for me, such as it was. On the rides home, sometimes we didn't speak at all. In those moments of resounding silence, our frustration spoke for us.

On weekends Eric went alpine skiing in the Laurentians. On holidays he went alpine skiing in Vermont. And Colorado. And Switzerland. On weekends and holidays I stayed home alone, reading course material, and laying the groundwork for a new and separate life.

After I moved to my new apartment near Mont Royal Park our paths crossed often, in many places, as if the force of our thoughts were pulling us to the same spot at the same time. Literally, our paths would cross on Mont Royal's walking paths. Our images would begin to crystallize against the panoramic views of the city; gaining form and substance the closer we approached. Once, Eric came walking towards me with a woman on his arm. They were engaged in animated conversation. They looked very relaxed together, and appeared to enjoy each other's company. The woman turned out to be Eric's sister, who was visiting from out of town. Eric did not attempt to avoid me. He came forward and was forthright, introducing me to his sister as "my student".

This situation continued for a year and a semester. Every time Eric felt me pulling away, he employed his vampiric charm to pull me back.

A fundraiser for the Institute was scheduled for December 5, 1991. Montreal entertainers were putting on a show for one evening at Centaur Theatre. Proceeds would go to the Institute. The tickets were seventy-five dollars each.

Everyone in class bought a ticket except me. When I was pressured to lend my "support", I responded, "You have my moral support."

Eric perceived that I could not afford the seventy-five dollar ticket. He offered to arrange a ticket for me. When I demurred he insisted, "Please. I want you with us." I don't know whether Eric paid for the ticket out of pocket or if it was a complimentary ticket. Besides leading courses at the Institute, Eric was on its board of governors. However the ticket was arranged, I accepted it.

Eric informed me that he would be picking me up at my apartment to drive "us" to the theatre, and it was understood that he would bring me back. It was going to be a long evening. Eric arrived at the entrance of my apartment building. His wife was in the front seat. I got into the back. In the theatre lobby, at the coat check, Eric handed me his wife's coat to hold while handing in his own. It was early winter, and already cold. We all wore heavy coats. I kept my coat on. I was angry.

Eric's wife had not acknowledged me in the car, but in the lobby of the theatre she scanned me and recalled, "Oh yes. I met you at that Holocaust thing." That Holocaust thing. In an instant, the guilt I felt at coveting this woman's husband was gone.

Inside the theatre I sat on one side of Eric, while his wife sat on the other. Resisting the temptation to hold my hand, Eric pressed his arm against mine, instead.

After the show there was a raffle draw. The prize was a weekend for two at a luxury downtown hotel. In an audience of over two hundred ticket holders, Eric won. He bounded onstage to claim his prize. A cheer rose for one of the Institute's most popular course leaders and governors. Eric graciously accepted the voucher that represented the prize, winked at the young female emcee who handed him the voucher and flirted, "Will you come with me?" Everyone laughed except me, and Eric's wife.

Eric was applauded all the way back to his seat, and that is where his social mask dropped. He pocketed the voucher. He did not look at his wife, and his wife did not look at him. I thought of how jubilant my father would've been to share such a gift with my mother. When I told my mother about this aspect of the evening she smirked, "He probably gave it to one of his kids."

A reception was held in the theatre lobby. Eric worked the room, and ignored me. It was a few moments to midnight, which meant it was a few moments to my birthday. I did not want to see in my birthday as the shit side of a triangle. I tried to signal Eric, even going so far as to gently rap on his back, but he refused to turn around, so I walked out of the reception area, went to a phone booth, and called a cab. Just after midnight, on a frosty night, I rode through the empty cobblestone streets of Montreal's Old City feeling as forlorn as Jane Eyre.

In the hiatus that divided the autumn semester from the winter one I sent a cheque to Eric for the amount of the ticket, along with a note apologizing for having accepted it. I believe I mailed the cheque to his home. It seemed more discreet than sending it to the Institute. Eric did not cash my cheque.

My mistake was to return for the winter semester. Eric continued to drive me home, but he invited another classmate to join us. In class he would sneer at my comments and dismiss my input. I had refused to keep the place Eric designated for me, and I was being punished.

It was on a bus one bitterly cold afternoon that winter when I found myself confronting Eric's wife, or being confronted by her. It took me by surprise. I didn't think women in her social position mingled with the masses on public transportation. Perhaps her car wouldn't start that day. Perhaps the lady didn't drive.

I was well bundled up against the cold, yet Ruth recognized me. She shivered, and she wasn't reacting to the cold. She appeared genuinely frightened. The smug Westmount matron whose coat I had carried, like a servant, was gone, and in her place sat an agitated woman edging old age.

It was clear that Eric had told her about me. Had she opened the envelope containing my cheque? In the reflection of Ruth's terrified look I saw the pathetic creature I felt I had become. It was hard for me to believe that she could perceive me as a serious threat.

While prolonging the agony of my doomed relationship with Eric I returned to my first love, the theatre, and the theatre was responding. It rescued me with the invitation to do a one-woman show. Accepting the offer meant I had no time nor energy for anyone nor anything else. I was grateful for the offer, and for the all-consuming work.

A month after the show ended I was scheduled to give a reading at The Jewish Public Library. Among the audience members was a man who would become a friend. He approached me after the reading with a broad smile and his arms extended. "You're wonderful!" That's how I met Michael. He was an English teacher at a local CEGEP. He was also a struggling poet. For the rest of that spring and throughout the summer, Michael and I continued the conversation begun at the library. We'd have long chats over the phone, or we'd meet and talk while strolling in local parks. After school and his teaching duties were done for the year Michael took on freelance work, ghost-writing for a wealthy businessman who intended to pass off the material as his own. Michael felt he was being underpaid. "But that's what he offered, and I didn't know how to ask for more. Still, he's a fascinating guy, though after our meetings I always feel slightly used. Though he doesn't pay much, he takes me to lunch, and he invites me up north to his country place. He's quite a specimen. The guy is in his early seventies, and in tip-top shape. The way he walks, I can barely keep up with him. He takes excellent care of himself. When he took me for lunch at *Kon Tiki* he ordered skinless broiled chicken, a dish of steamed vegetables, a bottle of mineral water, and that's all. Very disciplined. Very sharp. He's travelled extensively but then, he can afford to. Whenever I manage to work up the nerve to ask him for more money and am ready to do so, he launches into one of his fascinating tales. He's a great storyteller, and so hospitable that I feel greedy and guilty for even thinking of asking. He's a cultured guy, too, not just another Jewish businessman. He leads courses at The Thomas More Institute, the place where you took your first writing classes."

A bell went off. A light went on. It flashed in neon.

"Even if I am being used," Michael sighed, and continued, "I can't help liking the guy. He's got another side to him. A sensitive side. Sometimes he drifts off and starts talking about chivalric platonic love and telepathic communion between souls. He talks about souls who love each other yet can't be together. It's almost as if he's talking about a lost love."

I was quivering on the other end of the receiver. I WAS the receiver.

"Michael, what is the name of this charming rogue?"

I heard the name I expected to hear. "Oh Michael." My guard dropped, and my reserve broke. "Eric is speaking of me."

Michael gasped. I answered his unasked question. "No. We weren't lovers, though not because we didn't want to be."

However it ends, or whether it ends, the after-effects of unconsummated passion linger longer than a fully realized love. For the rest of that summer, vicariously I participated in the luncheon dates at upscale restaurants and sailed on the boat rides a ghost-writer enjoyed with his employer in the country, while Eric relayed messages of love he would never know were being delivered to me.

I would not see Eric again for a decade. During that decade I travelled as far and as often as resources allowed, I carried my dream of being an actress as far as it would go, I turned myself into a writer, and I learned to ski. (It was cross-country skiing that I learned, and I skied in small countries.) Eric flitted across my mind from time to time. I had a recurring dream that I was performing on stage and Eric was sitting in the audience, watching me.

Eric's wife Ruth died suddenly in 2003. After an appropriate interval Eric resurfaced socially with an age-appropriate widow, older than my mother yet younger than he, who had children of her own. She was a German Jewess who considered herself, and technically was, a Holocaust survivor. She reached Canada in 1940 and remembered, bitterly, the anti-Semitism that greeted her here. It is an odd perspective, considering what was going on in Europe, at the time. By the time Eric found his new companion my mother was on the verge of being diagnosed with cancer. This thunderclap transformed my priorities and turned me into a different person. My mother had become my partner, my child, and by default, the longest and most intimate relationship of my life. I had no patience for male charmers and their mind-bending games.

It was after Eric's wife died that our paths began crossing again. When I would see Eric with his lady friend, on occasion at Pollack Hall concerts, usually at Segal Centre theatre productions, I sometimes wondered what might've happened had his wife died ten years earlier. Would his children have eyed me warily, concerned over issues of inheritance? I might've been accused of being a gold digger. Certainly Jewish widows, with their casseroles at the ready, would've hissed viciously on seeing me assume what they would've considered their rightful place. Because Eric's feelings for me preceded his wife's passing, he might've felt guilty and become even nastier than he did. Would he have feared being ridiculed as an old fool? Would he have paraded me on his arm, proud of having acquired a significantly younger trophy companion, or would he have had me ducking under car seats? I don't believe he would've married me. Among Our Crowd, appearance is everything.

While I sat unobtrusively in a corner of the Segal Center lobby watching Eric, now in his eighties, still charismatic, still devilishly charming, grinning and glad-handing and working Our Crowd, I came to the conclusion that I had been spared.

Mostly Eric was unaware that he was under observation. After one performance I lingered in the lobby in order to greet a friend I spotted in the audience. Emerging into the lobby, Eric spotted me. He looked as alarmed as a deer caught in headlights. He swivelled in place, like a frenzied character in a cartoon. Then he took off through a back exit.

A time came when I was the one under observation. In October of 2010 I was scheduled to give a reading at the Eleanor London Library's Authors Salon. I was on the program with two other writers. One of them was Ursula F. Ursula was a ninety-year-old German Jewess who had written a memoir, and was heavily promoting it. She was involved with the Holocaust Center as a volunteer speaker. She was also a culture vulture. Her subscription tickets for the Segal Center fell on the same matinee as mine, and her seat was next to mine. We sat next to each other five times a year, for several years, before speaking. It was at a production of *Harvey* that I first spoke to Ursula. The stage was set in a living room, in America, in 1945. I turned to Ursula and asked, hoping I wasn't being offensive, "Is that what living rooms looked like in 1945?" Ursula was well preserved, but she was no spring chicken.

"I wouldn't know what a living room looked like in The States in 1945. I was in England at the time."

As Ursula spoke, I detected her German accent. A woman with a German accent who was in England in 1945? I reacted like a Geiger counter.

"I suppose you were on the *Kindertransport?*" The *Kindertransport* were the trains that brought German Jewish children to safety in England just before the start of the war.

"Why yes?! How did you know?"

I was my mother's daughter. How could I not know.

"It was an educated guess." From then on, Ursula and I greeted each other and shared our observations of the theatre productions as we sat side by side. I told my mother about my theatre companion.

"Of course I know Ursula! I interviewed her for *Living Testimonies*.[1] She's a very bright lady, but she's also highly

---

[1] McGill University's audio-visual history project. It filmed and preserves the testimonies of Holocaust survivors. The project predated Steven Spielberg's Shoah Foundation by five years. My mother was its associate director.

opinionated and feels superior to the rest of us. She's very full of herself. A typical German Jew."

I reported back to Ursula that we had my mother in common, though I edited my mother's feedback. Ursula had no memory of Mum. She simply couldn't remember her.

The library had done a professional job of promoting this event. I knew Ursula was participating, and I also knew that she did not identify the writer S. Nadja Zajdman with her seatmate Sharon at the Segal. Ursula had also done a professional job of promoting the event. A veritable crowd trooped in. It appeared as if the entire staff, along with the volunteers at the Holocaust Center, had been notified, and they were presenting themselves at the Authors Salon. Anyone connected with the Holocaust Center – with the exception of Ursula – knew my mother, and when they saw her sitting with me at a far corner in the back they greeted her.

"Renata! Hello! Have you come to hear Ursula read?"

"No!" My mother blasted, almost insulted by the suggestion. "I've come to hear my daughter read. This," my mother gestured, proudly presenting me, "is my daughter."

As the audience poured in, seating themselves at the chairs surrounding tables that were set up cabaret-style, I spotted an old familiar face. My heart leapt, and then it sank.

"Mum." Urgently, I whispered. "Eric is here."

Even after decades, there was no need to specify which, or what kind of Eric. As a woman wrote on the funeral parlour's website, he was "the legendary Eric".

"So? Big deal. Don't tell me he can still get to you after all this time. He's an old man!"

My sullenness said it all.

"Sweetheart, you go up there and give the beautiful reading you always give and let him look and screw him!"

Oh, Eric was prepared to look. Unlike Ursula, Eric had known me as "Nadja", not as "Sharon", and it wouldn't be hard to piece together the identity of S. Nadja Zajdman. Like the rest of the mob descending on the library, he had come to hear Ursula. I had seen them together in the Pollack Hall lobby along with his steady companion and several other ancients. I had seen them during intermissions, huddled together in conversation. The old and rich seem to travel in packs, like adolescent gangs. My mother told me that's because they need support holding each other up.

It may have been Ursula who invited Eric to the Authors Salon, but he knew he was going to see me. (On this particular evening, Eric showed up solo.) Knowing I would be trapped on stage, Eric was not shy about positioning himself at a table directly beneath the stage. He sat smack dab behind the center of the table, which would have allowed him to look up my skirt, had I been wearing one. He was protected behind the table, and I would be exposed up on stage. My recurring dream was being realized, and I didn't like it.

Ursula read first. Not only did she not respect the time limit allotted to each author, but after her reading she hogged the stage for a full half hour, cheerfully taking questions from the crowd. As the second writer approached the stage to begin her presentation, Ursula went behind a long table set up at the side of the hall. Copies of her book lay in stacks on the table, ready for sale. As the second writer began reading, Ursula began hawking her books. Loudly. Her friends and acolytes gathered around in animated conversation, ignoring the presentation being given onstage. The two young women in charge of organizing the event, members of library staff, looked on, seemingly helpless. Eric did not participate in this indecorous display. He remained rigidly in the seat he had claimed, abandoned at an emptied table. (The following year

I would be invited to read again at the Authors Salon. I was invited to read first. The sale of books was banned until all authors had given their readings.)

"This is outrageous!" My mother fumed. "I don't care if she is ninety and this is her Last Hurrah. You don't do that!"

As I watched Ursula holding court on one side of the auditorium while the hapless writer onstage struggled through her reading, I thought of how often and forcefully Ursula criticized the behaviour of students at the Segal Center matinees. She did not hesitate to chastise and scold, when she deemed it necessary, yet no one at this event dared confront Ursula and challenge her appalling exhibition.

"*Keine Kinderstube.*" Playfully I shook my head at my mother. It was a German expression Mum taught me, which she had learned from her mother. Loosely translated it means "No breeding. No class".

The writer scheduled to read second bore the brunt of Ursula and her acolytes' obnoxious display. By the time I was called up to read most of the offensive members of the audience had delivered their compliments, purchased their books, and left the hall. By the time I was introduced, there was only a scattering of people in the auditorium. Eric was one of them.

Though I have always read well, I still had not made the mental shift from actress to public speaker. I had not yet learned to control and dominate an unruly crowd. (I would learn. This experience taught me.) At that moment, I still believed the onus was on me to draw the audience in by the power of my performance. On that evening I succeeded, but I would never tolerate such rudeness again.

I read a story about my father. When I was done, as I was leaving the stage, I darted a quick glance at Eric. He was gazing at me softly. He appeared pensive, subdued, and impressed. Was he remembering the many evenings in class when he had called on me to read simply to hear the sound of my voice? I didn't know, and I cared even less.

The last time my path crossed Eric's was several seasons ago, at the Segal Center Theatre. He caught sight of me sitting in the front row next to Ursula. He scowled at me. It was a glare of terrible hostility. I was not only hurt; I was bewildered. I had as much right to be in the theatre, as he. Was I supposed to evaporate because my presence stirred up uncomfortable memories? I told my mother about it. She was incensed. "HE gave YOU a dirty look? What an asshole! He must be at least ninety. It's time for that guy to grow up!"

Eric was ninety then. Even he must've realized that he wasn't going to live forever. When we fall in love inappropriately we pick ourselves up and hope no one noticed. We can't always control the choices of our hearts. Eric didn't commit a crime and neither did I. The only one who got hurt was me.

In my heart I had forgiven Eric for being born too early. He might've forgiven me for being born too late. He might've given me one of those warm, wonderful smiles so vividly described on the condolence page of the funeral parlour's website. I would've been able to read it. A final smile would've told me, "Yes, I remember. I remember the life we lived during those car rides. I may still look good and I don't feel bad, but I've reached the exit. In the next life, if luck and timing fall on our side, I'll come back for you." But the chivalric Mr. P didn't smile. Instead he left me with a surly schoolboy scowl, and that last image of him is the one which remains.

Eric's last lady companion is acknowledged in his obituary. "He will be sadly missed and lovingly remembered by Anita H."

I don't, and won't miss Eric. I loved him, but I didn't

like him. I recall him with distaste. He was a lucky man who skied through life and when he fell, he landed in soft snow. I'm relieved he's gone. Or is he?

Eric's secret has died with him. Because I write, Eric's secret may not die with me.

SUMMER, 2015

INTENSIVE CARE

He was born in Joliet, Quebec, early in 1926. He had an unremarkable childhood, and came of age listening to Rene Levesque's Radio-Canada broadcasts from a newly liberated Europe. With a marked distaste for organized religion in a province dominated by the Catholic Church, his options were few. He chose to become a doctor.

It would be as a young general practitioner dispensing tranquilizers to burdened housewives compelled to bear too many children, that he discovered his gift for healing wounded souls. By the simple act of listening to his patients and receiving what they had to say, the G.P. noticed that they began feeling better even before they filled his prescriptions. Fascinated by this phenomenon, he decided to further explore it. At the age of twenty-eight, handicapped by a severely limited knowledge of English, he applied as a mature student to Harvard's medical school in the department of psychiatry. The G.P. from Joliet was accepted.

On his first night at Harvard, he went to take a shower in the communal washroom, inadvertently walking in on a nude female student. Though limited, Liard's English was still better than the Harvard administration's French, and he guessed what led to the mix-up. He had been billeted in the women's dormitory. The English translation of his name was John. In French, it is spelled JEAN. He remembered the documents in his room, which would prove his identity. In an attempt to communicate with the distraught young woman, Jean from Joliet carefully and haltingly iterated, "Come to my room. I want to show you something." The terrified female was hysterical now. Jean retreated to his room – without taking a shower. The next morning he contacted the administration, and was quickly transferred to the men's dorm.

After completing his course of studies, Dr. Jean Liard returned to Quebec fluently bilingual, with a degree in psychiatry, and an American bride. He took up residency at The Montreal General Hospital, and twenty years later confessed to me that he had been compelled to witness, though he never actively participated in administering electric shock treatments. He was repelled by the procedure, and embarrassed that he had even a peripheral part in them.

As Dr. Liard's medical career progressed, he was invited to sit on advisory boards where colleagues would pontificate. "Neurotics are too difficult to treat. It's best to break them down and make them schizophrenic so we can prescribe Librium." Dr. Liard didn't last long in these settings. An iconoclast ahead of his time he would, over time, withdraw, walk out, and resign in disgust. He opened his own practice under Quebec's newly established Medicare plan, and that is how I met him in August of 1976.

I was sent to Dr. Liard after a suicide attempt, precipitated by a therapist's repeated sexual abuse. Eating disordered and in an emotionally fragile state, I had been taken to this fashionable therapist, who began molesting me under the guise of treatment. As my parents paid his bills, he would report to them that I was frigid.

The summer when I was four, during an extended stay on the farm of our next-door neighbours, Mr. and Mrs. Trautmann, I knew enough to run and scream at the top of my lungs, "Eric tried to pull my panties down!" I also knew to run for protection to the men, not to the women. By the time I was twenty, I had been civilized and subdued into a paralytic silence.

After I cut my wrists, the offending therapist tossed me to Dr. Liard. After the assessment, Dr. Liard decided that I was to come in for sessions three times a week. He half-reassured and half-reprimanded my frightened parents,

"That girl is saner than ninety-nine per cent of the shrinks I know. She's just very confused – and I don't blame her!" Much later he would tell me, "When you first walked in you were dishevelled and distraught, but I could see that the eye of the storm is calm."

Though I didn't recognize it at the time, Dr. Liard's leading questions were meant to ferret out a sense of self-loathing I believed no one had ever suffered, except me. After the first week in treatment I told my mother what had taken place in the therapist's office. I felt Dr. Liard needed to know – as if he hadn't guessed – but I was unable to bring myself to tell him directly, so I sent my parents instead.

At the appointment I avoided, my parents asked Dr. Liard if they should instigate legal proceedings against my molester. He advised against it. "Your daughter isn't strong enough to withstand a court case. The law is slanted in favour of the perpetrator. A legal proceeding would destroy her. I'll fix that bastard in my own way. She's more important than he is. My mission is to save her life."

Liard kept his word. When the therapist's lease in the medical building came up for renewal, Liard organized a posse of neighbouring doctors and let the landlord know that they would relocate *en masse* if the therapist's lease was renewed. The therapist left; the doctors stayed.

When I returned for the next appointment, Liard's sole reference to the revelations I had transmitted through my parents was oblique. "If someone throws dirt on you, it isn't your dirt. You can always take a shower and become clean."

At the end of the session, he idled in the doorway of his office. I would come to recognize it as his signature stance. "By the way," Liard remarked, too casually. Then his bulbous blue eyes, like searchlights, bored into mine. He cocked an eyebrow, and a hint of a grin played across his moustache-framed mouth. "Did I pass?"

In response, I lowered my gaze and gave him a shy and grudging smile.

After my first year in treatment, my father mused, "I used to think psychiatrists were for crazy people. Now I see that they're really for sensitive people – to learn how to deal with crazy people!"

Quebec Medicare covered only one year of psychiatric treatment. In the summer of 1977 my parents asked Dr. Liard how they could continue paying him. "Don't worry," he grinned at my mother, with his customary twinkle. "I'll use your card for a year, then I'll take your husband's card, and then I'll use your son's card. I'll make you all sick!"

Jean Liard was short, for a man. I remember him standing five feet six inches. He had a thick mass of wavy hair, originally dark, which looked like a chef had been too liberal with a salt shaker. A moustache in the same salt and pepper tones framed a mouth that appeared constantly poised to break into a grin. He smoked cigarettes and made singular fashion statements. In spring he sported tan-coloured slacks and a loud plaid jacket. In summer he donned white sneakers and a scarlet-red suit with a matching red tie that looked like a flashing exclamation mark.

Not surprisingly, Liard's role models were comedians. He made a point of letting me know, "The people I remember with the greatest affection are the people who have made me laugh. People who make us laugh are worthy of memory."

He held Bob Hope in high esteem because, for decades, Hope sacrificed a comfortable Christmas at home with family in order to entertain the young and scared and lonely stationed overseas. He made a study of the late-night television talk show host Johnny Carson. He countered my derisive reaction with, "Do you think it's easy to invite in strangers, seat them on a couch, and then make them feel so comfortable that they'll reveal their secrets to you? Think about it. Carson makes it look easy, but it's not as easy as it looks."

I thought about it. Then I went home and thought about it. Again.

My jaunty doctor sparkled when he spoke and glowed when he moved. His smile was sly, his laugh was a shout of delight, and there appeared always to be a hint of mischief in his pale, bulbous eyes.

This shining diamond seemed to have cultivated a persona akin to Peter Falk's television detective Colombo, a character at the height of its popularity during that period. Liard knew, before you did, where the bodies were buried and who had murdered the victims, but with his light-hearted, almost absent-minded air, he would coax the hidden culprits into consciousness.

During the first year in treatment, I began to write. This time, I wasn't writing to please my English teachers. I was writing because, if I didn't write, I was going to eat and eat and eat. I was writing in order to safely express my rage and my anguish, instead of stuffing them down. I was writing to pacify my ravaged spirit. I was writing to save my sanity.

As I wrote, often in the middle of a sleepless night, I gave myself one proviso. Whatever I wrote, I would then destroy. This decision won me the freedom to write without self-censorship.

After months of intense literary outpouring I discovered that I was beginning to write coherently, even eloquently. I then gave myself permission to save these passages in a notebook. I had inadvertently and organically begun a journal.

In the autumn of 1977, I went overseas for the first time. From London, I wrote Liard a long letter. Upon my return, he raved about it.

"I showed it to my wife! I showed it to my children! I

told them, 'You must read this! It's from a patient who is simply describing what she sees, and it's as if we're right there with her, seeing it too!' " Liard dubbed me "the 20th century de Sevigny" in reference to the 17th century French aristocrat whose letters were celebrated for their vividness and wit.

At the end of the session, at the door, I stopped, hesitated, and shyly asked, "Would you like to see some of the other stuff I wrote?"

Liard hooted in triumph. His bulbous eyes appeared to bug out of his head. "Well what do you think I've been hinting at all morning!"

A morning appointment was atypical. Most of my appointments were set at the end of the day in order to accommodate my father, who drove me to them at the end of his workday. Dr. Liard never prescribed medication. He used his prescription pad only to note down appointment times. He disregarded the hour limit set by Quebec Medicare, and gave his patients all the time they needed. I always had a book with me, while waiting my turn, and I never minded the wait. My father would sit and wait with me, and then he would sit and wait for me. When I emerged, sometimes after a three-hour session, we would go out for a leisurely dinner, in order to give me time to decompress. I cherished the private time these circumstances afforded with my father as much as I valued my sessions with Liard. I would never again love, nor be loved, by such sterling men.

When Dr. Liard read my journal entries he said, "Your writing is mature, but you are not. You'll have to grow into your talent." Dr. Liard became convinced that I would become a writer. He bore witness to my return to classes, my first job, and my foray into professional theatre. All the while he burbled and believed, "I have the best of both worlds here in my office, because I get to enjoy your physical expressiveness, the sound of your voice, and I am an audience to your ideas. It would be a gift to the public if you would combine these things. Perhaps, one day, you'll merge your acting with your writing talent. Perhaps, one day, you'll be performing your own words."

These days, when I find myself at a podium, on a stage, on the verge of giving a literary reading, I see my Colombo-of-the-soul shifting in his swivel chair. "Is this what you meant?" I address my blithe spirit, now resident in a parallel universe. "Is this what you saw for me?"

I was three years into treatment when Liard transferred his practice to a small room with a separate entrance in the basement of his new home. In this space serving as an office, a long and wide picture window looked out onto a body of water. The water was ringed by virgin wilderness. Liard called the water a river, but it may have been a lake. Two identical swivel chairs furnished the space. Liard claimed the chair close to the window, and patients were relegated to the chair that I came to call The Hot Seat. The house seemed to have leapt off the cover of Home Beautiful Magazine. It was located on a secluded island across the bridge from Dollard des Ormeaux. Ile Bizard, or Buzzard's Isle, as Liard loved to call it, was still a well-kept secret enjoyed by the privileged few. Liard seemed to need to explain to me how a doctor working under the financial constraints of socialized medicine was able to acquire such a find. My psychiatrist confided to me that, years earlier, he had a patient who epitomized a modern-day Job. He was a businessman who had gone bankrupt. His wife left him, taking their children with her. The man was despondent. He became suicidal.

Dr. Liard offered the patient a sum of money to restart his business on condition that he accept it as a gift, and not as a loan. "Once the funds are transferred, they become yours. You are not allowed to pay me back." The patient accepted Liard's gift, and restarted his business. The new business boomed. The patient became a multi-millionaire. He remarried, and started a new family.

When he was fully on his feet, the grateful patient turned the tables on Dr. Liard. He offered to make him a gift of a luxury home, and to set up a trust fund for his children. Liard knew not only how to give, but he knew to do what is harder, which is to receive. Dr. Liard and his family were secure for life.

I was amazed. I was also mystified. "Just like that? You gave him the money and everything turned around for him? Why did you insist on giving him the money? Why didn't you just give him a loan?"

Patiently, Liard explained. "By its nature, a loan creates stress. As soon as a person accepts a loan he is under pressure to pay it back. The man had lost everything. He couldn't handle more stress. What he needed was someone to believe in him. Making a gift of the money gave him the confidence to believe in himself."

What was it that Dr. Liard saw in me? I was on the cusp of womanhood. He would keep me for hours after the official end of our sessions, filling me with stories of his life and experiences. Why did he pour so much of himself into me? It seemed as if, like my father, he subconsciously felt a sense of urgency in preparing me for a future he wasn't going to see.

Leaning back in his swivel chair to admire the wild beauty of the body of water flowing virtually at his feet, Liard revelled in his self-created role as an eccentric psychiatrist ensconced on "Buzzard's Isle". Approaching his mid-fifties, Liard had it made. His marriage was happy and his children were well adjusted. His work was meaningful, and the good he had done was rewarding him tenfold. Indeed, the doctor had everything. He had everything except time.

During the third year of treatment I had a stunningly vivid dream. I was standing in a darkened room, dressed in black. People dressed in white surrounded me. They milled around the room, conversing with each other, but I stood still and alone, as if enveloped in a placenta. I stood staring at a long and wide object. It was a coffin, and Dr. Liard was in it.

I was deeply disturbed by this dream. I wasn't sure I would divulge it to Liard. Ultimately I did, and my premonition was dismissed. "It doesn't mean anything. You're just afraid of losing me." This was true, as far as it went. In the same year, Liard quit smoking cold turkey. He made the effort too late.

Life seemed to accelerate during that last good year. My mother asked to be taken on by Dr. Liard. When I made the request, he hooted, "Ho ho! Mother AND daughter, eh? Well, if you can handle it, I can!"

My laconic younger brother, who kept his own counsel and went his own way, startled us all when he announced that he was considering becoming a psychiatrist, and would Dr. Liard see him for a consultation on the matter? Introducing my brother to the psychiatrist I watched, with amusement, as his confidence turned to discomfort when he realized that he was about to enter The Hot Seat. Liard darted a barely perceptible glance at me, and I knew to remove myself to the waiting room.

No matter what progress I made, Liard would not consider his work complete until he saw me, literally, in the driver's seat. I had always been afraid of learning to drive. During the fourth year of treatment, I learnt. Still, I was afraid to drive as far as Ile Bizard. In the summer of 1980, I drove to Ile Bizard.

It was the first week of August. People were on vacation

and traffic was light. The night before my appointment I took my father's car and drove along the 2 and 20 Highway, across the West Island and over the bridge that spans Rivière-des-Prairies. I timed the drive, and then gave myself extra time the following day.

The afternoon of my appointment was picture perfect. Soft cottony clouds scudded across a block of solid blue sky. The mid-summer sun blazed, and the grass on Liard's lawn shimmered like emerald threads.

Liard came into the waiting room to greet me, costumed in his merry red suit. Atypically, he was on time. No one else emerged from his office, and we were alone in the waiting room. I appeared to be the only patient he was seeing that day.

Mischievously, he looked around. He even looked under the cushions of the chairs. I stifled a guffaw.

"Your father's not here."

I was prepared to play. "No, he's not."

"Your brother's not here?"

"No. Just me." My grin grew wider. So did Liard's.

"How did you get here – by helicopter?"

I pointed towards the entrance. My father's car was parked outside. Liard's grin grew as wide as the grin on Lewis Carroll's Cheshire Cat.

Good. Good." He tilted his head towards the open door of his office. "Come in."

At the end of the session we stood at a small table situated in the corner away from the window. It held little more than pens and a prescription pad on which to note appointment reminders. Liard told me he was going to take a break for the rest of the summer, and gave me an appointment for after Labour Day. He had never taken off so much time before, but I thought nothing of it. Standing at the desk with my appointment reminder in hand, I repeated a question I had asked in many ways, many times before. "Why does it work between us?"

We were standing side by side. Without facing me, Liard responded quietly, "It's because we love each other."

After the session Liard did something he had never done with me. He came outside to see me off. I believe he did it in order to witness what was, for him, the culmination of a four-year investment of heart and soul and raw psychic energy. Liard beamed with satisfaction as I approached my father's car, opened the door on the driver's side and entered, alone. As I started the engine and pulled away, Liard remained on the sidewalk and waved. Through the rear view mirror I watched Liard watching me. In his silly red suit he looked like a jolly summer Santa. His receding figure kept waving until both he and I were out of each other's sight. I had no way of knowing, though he may have suspected, that we would never see each other again.

A week before my next appointment, in early September, we received a call from Mrs. Liard. Dr. Liard was cancelling and would be suspending all appointments until further notice. No explanation was given.

The call was unsettling. I had assumed that when he deemed me ready Liard would lift his wing, nudge me out of his nest, and I would fly into the sweet promise of a good and happy life.

It was a Saturday afternoon, close to October. The fields of tall beige grasses that waved outside my window had been razed and replaced by a commercial complex. It was one of the first indoor shopping malls, and from all over the city people were flocking to my suburban neighbourhood to experience this new concept in all-weather shopping.

I was restless. Liard was constantly on my mind. I bolted the apartment and headed to the mall. There was nowhere else to go.

At the entrance of the shopping center, a petite blonde woman and her dark-haired daughter confronted me. It was Mrs. Liard and her daughter Monique. The encounter was a shock for all of us, but not surprising to me. I felt as if the force of my thoughts had summoned them.

Mrs. Liard was caught off guard, and blurted information she had been instructed not to reveal. Dr. Liard had lung cancer.

In the ensuing year I soldiered on, my days dulled by depression and my nights haunted by hallucinatory dreams. Within that year my father convinced my mother to allow me to leave home and live on my own. Then he helped me to do so.

Dr. Liard had no back-up and made no provisions for his vulnerable patients. We were shut out of his dying and cut loose to find our own way. He proved human, after all.

On Remembrance Day of 1981, my parents were in a lawyer's office, when my mother suddenly blanched. My frightened father clasped her hands. "What's wrong, my darling, what is it?!"

"He's calling!" He's calling!" My mother managed to gasp.

"I don't understand!" My father was alarmed. "What are you trying to say?"

"He's trying to reach us! He's calling! He's calling!"

Later, when she was able, my mother explained. "As Daddy was speaking, his voice seemed to change. His voice changed into Liard's voice. Liard's voice was coming out of Daddy's mouth. It got louder and louder and I knew what he was trying to say." Liard's departed spirit used my parents as a channel for the message he had to convey. The next morning my mother checked the newspaper for confirmation, and found it in the obituary section. The day before she heard his voice, Dr. Liard died.

There was no funeral. Liard had specified that his body be cremated. Before the cremation, a three-day wake was held in a West Island funeral parlour. The morning of November 12 heralded the last day of the wake. I was granted just enough time to say good-bye. My dad drove me to my final appointment with Dr. Liard.

It wasn't late, but it was so very dark. At the end of a dimly lit room stood Liard's closed coffin. A black and white studio photograph of him perched on its lid. My father held back, hat in hand, a supportive shadow hovering between the entrance and the hall. I entered the hall and approached the coffin. I wore a long-sleeved, black woollen sheath. The other mourners wore light-coloured clothing. I stood alone and trembling, in the manifestation of my worst nightmare, up until that time. Then I found a stool in a corner and crumpled onto it, isolated in a bubble of heartache.

Dr. Liard's son André approached. He was taller than his father and his hair was dark, but he had the same luminous, lamp-like eyes. He knelt next to me and offered, "My father thought a lot of you. He believed in your potential." André Liard had just lost his father, he was younger than I was, and he was comforting me.

"Did you resent the extra time he spent with me?" I felt miserable and guilty.

"Well, sometimes it got a bit much." André was trying to be kind, but he couldn't deny it. "After you would leave he'd come in for supper. We tried to hold supper for him, but usually it had grown cold. Dad was drained. It was an effort for him to eat. It was an effort for him to speak. We'd look at him and shake our heads. Then he'd defend himself, 'Well, I can't help it! The more she talks, the better she gets!'" At this reminiscence, we were able to smile.

My dad and I stayed at the wake as long as Liard's family did. We walked together behind his coffin.

On the ride home my dad gripped the steering wheel, battling against tears that threatened to blind him.

"That man wasn't meant for a family." I sat mute in my sorrow. "That man was meant for the world."

In our mutual, quiet grief, it was my father who fathomed the depth of my pain. Always gentle and patient, in the aftermath of Liard's death he watched over me the way he had when I was a child. He instructed his secretary, "Whenever my daughter calls, you come and get me. Wherever I am, no matter what I'm doing, I'm never too busy for my daughter."

Eighteen months after Liard's passing my father, too, was dead. I was twenty-seven years old, and I had lost them both.

Today, Liard's beloved Buzzard's Isle is a wealthy enclave serving as home and playground to provincial politicians and local sports celebrities. Their yachts cruise the lake in summer. Their mansions are too closely spaced. There is one street name that feels familiar, and I ride down its road, which leads to the lake. If Liard's home is still standing, I am unable to identify it.

On the far side of the marina and its traffic there is a nature park. It is a vast expanse of enchantment winding its way through glades of maples and cedars and pines. I visit all year round. In winter, I ski there. I pick mushrooms in autumn, and wildflowers in spring. As I hike through its trails I hear the light-hearted tone of Liard's tenor, long-stilled. "I am like a guide in the woods. I walk ahead, forging a trail and clearing the brambles, so that you can come straight on through."

It is in nature that the eye of the storm reclaims its calm. It is in the woods of Ile Bizard where I find consolation and peace.

Jean Liard
Born January (24, 25, 26?), 1926
Died November 10, 1981
Worthy of Memory

SUMMER, 2013

FINDING MY FEET

In the early autumn of 2016, I joined a hiking club. My intention was to find a way into nature. I don't own a car. The most I hoped for was to sit quietly on the school bus as it transported our group of active senior citizens into the countryside. I still pay full price for everything, so I don't know how I've come to be considered a senior citizen, but in certain milieu, I am. Perhaps I am a junior senior.

On that first Friday morning I arrived at the meeting point. A member of the club noticed me hanging back in a corner, clutching my new knapsack. I was more nervous that morning than on my first day of kindergarten. "Come on in!" She called. "The water's fine!"

At eight-thirty on Friday mornings we were ready to roll. At two o'clock on Friday afternoons we hauled our exhausted carcasses back onto the bus. Ouf!

On the bus, I discovered that I could comfortably socialize. On the trails, I was startled to discover how frightened I had become of downward slopes. As I stiffened and inched along, a hand reached from behind, gently nudging the back side of my forearm and guiding my direction. "Why are you afraid?" The warm male voice of one of the fitness trainers who lead these outings asked. Why, indeed? I came to think of these trainers as good shepherds and shepherdesses who will not allow a lamb to slip over the side of a hill. Beguiled by the beauty of the views, at first I moved forward tentatively, later with budding assurance. And though I sometimes tripped over the exposed root of an ancient maple, I was always grateful to be out in nature breathing cedar-scented air. Lunchtime would find me stretched out on a rock or a dock or a picnic bench by a rushing gorge or a sun-dappled lake.

When autumn turned to winter, we strapped snowshoes onto our boots, and the lunches we carried in our knapsacks were consumed in huts, by the amber-coloured flames of logs burning in wood stoves. The first time I put on snowshoes, I felt like I would topple over.

"Stomp, Sharon, stomp your feet!" The head shepherdess instructed. "The reason you feel like you're falling is because you aren't stepping forcefully. The snowshoes have clamps. They'll bite the ground and hold you up. Stomp, Sharon! Stomp!" So I stomped and I clomped, feeling like The Abominable Snowman. Climbing uphill was hard, but not frightening. The effort felt familiar. In a sense, I've been climbing uphill all my life.

Sometimes we tramped in open meadows surrounded by taupe-coloured trees, and sometimes we edged our way through narrow paths in a snow-laden glade I dubbed The Land of Sugar-Frosted Pines. Once, we entered a region in the Laurentians called Farhills. These hills were not only far, but steep. On one hill, all my fellow hikers had to be helped down the icy and treacherous trail, so what chance did I have? When my turn came, I gauged the conditions and made my choice. "Screw this." A fine line separates courage from stupidity, and I was on the verge of crossing it. I plunked down onto the ground, raised my snow-shoe clad feet in the air, tossed my hiking sticks away from me, shoved at the snow with my gloves, and whizzed down the slope, the ice under my bottom turning me into a human toboggan. Two alarmed shepherdesses dashed down the hill – they were the only ones capable of doing so. "Sharon! Are you alright?!"

I thrust out my arms and through crystallized breath exulted, "It's the only way to travel!"

Having flown down the hill literally by the seat of my pants, I faced another challenge. How to stand up? My feet flailed in the air. They were trapped in the snowshoes.

"I need to get these things off." I assumed.

"No you don't," the shepherdesses corrected. "We'll get you on your feet."

"You can't!" I bleated. "I'm too heavy."

"Oh yes we can!" Shepherdess Annette positioned herself on one side of me. Shepherdess Annie positioned herself on the other. "As we lift, you push. Push from your knees, Sharon! Push!" So saying, they heaved, I ho-ed, and up I sprang! I grinned at the good shepherdesses in admiration and awe. Not only was I on my feet; I was also smiling.

By late afternoon we were back in the city. I returned to my apartment, soaked in a warm, sea-salted bath, and in sweet exhaustion fell into bed. My body burned, my muscles ached, and I slept like one of the logs that occasionally blocked our paths on the hiking trails.

WINTER, 2017

MOUNTAIN GUIDE

I was sitting by the gas-lit fireplace in my local library when a book on the table caught my eye. It was the collected correspondence of the novelist Marjorie Rawlings and her editor, Maxwell Perkins. As I read their letters I could hear their long-stilled voices speaking to each other, and to me, across the expanse of decades. I tried to check out the book, but was told it was a reject from a book sale, and if I wanted it I would have to buy it. So I did.

At home, I looked up Maxwell Perkins on the Internet. A link led me to Perkins' granddaughter, the novelist Ruth King Porter, who lived in rural Vermont. Ruth was giving away her novels, asking nothing in return but that readers post reviews on her website. I sent for Ruth's books, and a correspondence began. Soon, we wanted to meet in person. I scheduled a visit to Ruth in spring; then her mother's dying began. I rescheduled in autumn; then my mother's dying began. Instantly I cancelled travel plans and let go of my already-purchased bus ticket, but a friend with a car offered to take me on a shorter day trip to Vermont. Encouraged by my mother, I accepted.

"We are two middle-aged women, both wearing glasses." I told Ruth. "My friend is a blonde with dark roots. I still think of myself as brunette, but there is more salt than pepper in my hair, now." Ruth wrote that she would be waiting for me under the clock tower of Montpelier's City Hall. I knew what Ruth looked like from the photographs on her website.

We rode into Montpelier on a gloriously warm day at high noon. I saw Ruth sitting on a bench under the clock tower, scribbling in a notebook. Main Street was packed with tourists, and we couldn't stop the car in front of City Hall. We found a parking space down the street. My friend waited in the car, while I ran down the block. "Ruth?" The woman on the bench looked up, and then leapt up.

Ruth was a pre-hippie Back-to-the-Lander, in her early seventies when I first met her. At our first encounter, she wore a white work shirt, faded blue jeans, and a black money belt slung over her shoulder. She walked like someone who rode horses.

"Where's your friend?" Ruth called through the crowd of tourists blocking the sidewalk.

"She's waiting in the car!" I called back. I led Ruth to the car and the friend in it. Ruth led us both on a tour of the golden-domed state capital building.

"I hope we don't run into my son." Ruth twinkled. "He'd be embarrassed by the way I'm dressed. My son Louis works as an aide to the governor." When the tour was over Ruth led the way in her battered old car out of Montpelier and higher into the Green Mountains, where another world awaited.

Ruth's husband Bill and a second son, Robbie, rode their tractors out of the woods to greet us on the porch of a rambling farmhouse. Nearby, three large dogs stiffened in alert: Ellie and Flora danced in attendance to the top dog, Chief. Ruth's daughter Molly, an artist who lived, Thoreau-like, in a cabin she built with her hands, bounded up a hill to join us. The open and friendly faces of Ruth's family smiled at me kindly. I'm sure they were aware of my situation, though no one referred to it. Taught, lean, Alabama-born Bill wiped the grime off his hands and stepped forward to shake mine. I felt as though I'd stepped into an illustration by Norman Rockwell.

As early darkness fell my companion and I crossed back over the border, returning to Montreal and my mother's apartment. "Hello sweetheart." My dying mother smiled tenderly. "How did it go with the lady in Vermont?"

What could I say? I felt guilty at having left her, even

for a few hours. I didn't feel like relaying the details of an excursion to Vermont.

Six months later I returned to Montpelier by bus, alone. Once more, Ruth met me under the clock tower. For a few days I curled under Ruth's wing, sunning on her roof, sleeping in Max Perkins' bed, waking to birdsong and skimming the staggering array of autographed out-of-print books dedicated by grateful authors to their engaged and caring editor. "Grieving is hard work," Ruth would say in greeting when, after a nap, I descended a steep staircase into her dark country kitchen. As we stood side by side in the verdant meadow which was her front yard, Ruth added, as much in amazement as in sorrow, "A year ago this time, both our mothers were alive."

Ruth King Porter is an American blueblood whose antecedents hark back to a woman who held a door open for George Washington. I am the Canadian-born daughter of refugees. My mother, a woman who survived three invasions and fell into the category of less than one per cent of children under the age of fifteen who survived the infamous Warsaw Ghetto, later in life became a pioneer in Holocaust education. Many people find my mother's story repellent and turn away from any mention of it, whereas Ruth and her husband Bill were fascinated. Ruth did for me what I had done for my mother: she listened. And she encouraged me to tell my mother's story.

Six months after my first extended stay, I was back on the farm. Ruth and Bill acknowledged what would have been my mother's birthday by lighting large candles in a spectacularly tangled chandelier made entirely of logs. Through the wall-sized picture window we watched the cold autumn rain and wind lash the last leaves off a forest full of trees. As we ate hot squash and a pot full of peas grown in Ruth's garden, the lit log chandelier shone, the tree-bark-shaded lamps glowed, and the wood stove burned.

    I went back to Ruth and Bill's farm several times after that. In between visits Ruth did for me what her grandfather did for Ernest Hemingway, F. Scott Fitzgerald, Thomas Wolfe, and Marjorie Rawlings; she wrote to me and elicited writing from me, read and critiqued my material, encouraged, cajoled, indicated where and when she believed I veered off-track, and gently nudged me back. Clutching the psychic lifeline tossed to me by the descendant of a legendary literary editor, I lived and worked alone and in growing peace in my suburban Montreal apartment, producing a memoir of my mother. My mother knew that my writing would sustain me after she was gone. Ruth Porter's mentorship sustained me during the darkest days of my life.

––––––––––

WINTER, 2018

EUREKA SPRINGS REVISITED

In early November, I spent two serendipitous days in the tiny resort town of Eureka Springs, located in the Ozarks, at the edge of Arkansas. I had accepted an invitation from a friend in the American Midwest to join her on her ranch in Kansas, and she was taking me on a road trip. Since we would be riding through Missouri, I asked if I might see something connected with Mark Twain. "Hannibal is on the other side of the state." I was mildly disappointed. However, as a Canadian and an easterner I found everything exotic, so I decided to sit back and surrender to whatever wanted to present itself to me.

Hitting the trail, we headed south into a prolonged autumn. To my wonder and delight, our road led to a winding path that cut a swath up hills and down dales, deep into a forest fiery with colour. The trees seemed ablaze, but it was a safe and cool fire. Even more astonishing to me was the sign that loomed on the horizon proclaiming, "Mark Twain National Forest". My wish had been granted, after all.

We reached our destination in mid-afternoon. A week before, the clocks were turned back an hour. (In Kansas, the clock seems stuck in the 1950s.) By the time we checked into the Basin Park Hotel, dusk was descending over this hamlet nestled in the mountains. In the shadows of a short November day I strolled along the main street, called Spring. A warm orange sun was sinking into a cool lavender sky. Turning a corner, with the deep purple of the mountains as backdrop, a machine pumping soap bubbles had been set at the entrance of a retro dress shop. Transparent balloons lifted into the dimming sky as the sound of Glenn Miller's sweet swing poured out of its doorway, like buckwheat honey.

Perusing the storefronts of Spring Street, I was attracted

to the window of a hotel called The New Orleans. I walked into a lobby resplendent with dark oak panelling, fake palm trees, and silent ceiling fans. I entered into conversation with the woman at the reception desk, who spoke like a Kennedy. She was originally from Boston. Her husband's work had brought her to Arkansas. The move, for her, was a reluctant one. She was a cultured woman, and had anticipated being stranded in a hillbilly wilderness. Instead she found herself cocooned in Shangri-La. When I told her I was a writer from Canada she informed me that the town housed a writer's colony, called Dairy Hollow. I understood what drew me to this hotel. I would visit the colony the next day.

Back at our hotel, my hostess and companion had arranged a private suite for me. The Basin Park Hotel was founded in 1905. It is built into the side of a mountain. The hotel has played host to gangsters, high-rolling gamblers, and movie stars. Now it was sheltering me. It is rumoured that the rooms are haunted by the ghosts of guests who have passed on to The Other Side.

The suite assigned to me was massive. So was the bed. The mattress was soft and lumpy. Perhaps Al Capone's sister left impressions on it. During the Depression, she was stashed away in this hotel. The *fin-de-siècle* bathroom wasn't user-friendly. A large round table, surrounded by high-backed gilded chairs, was set against the window overlooking the illuminated lamps along Spring Street. Here a jazz-age gangster might've enjoyed intimate *téte-à-tétes* with his wasp-waisted, helmet-haired moll, and there seemed no better place to sup, but my hostess Bo insisted on eating out, so we went down to the bar, empty on this off-season Tuesday evening, installed ourselves in a booth in an alcove, and ate our meal accompanied by the soundtrack of an ancient Andy Griffith episode, which droned on the TV hanging beside beer glasses on a wall.

During dinner I picked up a brochure lying next to the ketchup bottle. I discovered that a room with a jacuzzi cost the same as my assigned suite. After dinner I went down to the reception desk, requested, and was granted a change of rooms. In exchange for space, I received luxury. My new room was intimate and cosy. The amenities of the early 21rst century were creatively tucked away in the ambiance of the turn of the 20th. The mattress of the queen-sized bed was solid and firm. There were not one, but two bathrooms. The bathroom to the left was the original, installed in 1905. Crossing the room, with its ersatz chintz lampshades and upholstery, its early 20th century washbasin sustained by early 21rst century plumbing, I opened the door to the second bathroom and stepped into a hedonistic heaven. The gleaming white room was dominated by the most ergonometically perfect jacuzzi I have ever experienced. Gleefully I retrieved a bath pillow from my carry-on case, stripped, eased my aching back into the water, switched on the jets and invisible fingers, strategically placed, massaged me while I soaked for over an hour. Outside the opaque, oval-shaped window, a sliver of moon was slung low over silent Spring.

In the morning I was back in the tub. Despite the opacity of the window the sun was shining through, its beams dancing on the bath water and warming my face. In November.

Bo spent the morning souvenir-hunting, and I set off to explore Dairy Hollow, the colony housed at the edge of a forest, at the end of Spring. We met again at noon. Bo had been busy that morning. Besides trolling the shops, she had been scouting the restaurants, and discovered a hole in the wall that had won the New York Times' food critics' award. It is called The Oasis, and it is located at the top of the second stairway after the curve in the road. The owner doubles as chef, and her son serves as the establishment's sole waiter. Maria cooks up creative Mexican cuisine, with vegetarian options. She cooks from scratch, and she does it every day.

In the afternoon Bo and I separated for a siesta. In the evening we met in the corridor; we were heading for The Pine Mountain Jamboree.

Bo drove us to the outskirts of town – the outskirts of town being ten minutes away. Against the blackness of a November night there stood a snow-white cottage. It looked like a layer of a wedding cake. In front of a long French window, a fake white Christmas tree was perched on its porch. White-haired people were gathering inside. We climbed the porch steps, and joined them. Silver chandeliers tinkled. Their tiny bulbs blazed. Behind long tables laid out in rows, sellers were hawking souvenirs; pink-coloured soap bars carved into the shape of hearts, colognes, and CDs of the music we were about to hear. At the entrance of the auditorium, behind a large counter, white corn kernels were being heated and popped in bulk. A warm, buttery smell wafted through the air. The popcorn was being handed out in red-and-white striped boxes, and it was on the house.

We took our boxes of popcorn and exited the lobby, into the auditorium. The audience seemed a sea of bobbing white-haired heads. Groups of seniors had been bussed in for the jamboree. The show began sedately, with slow, reverential, white gospel music. Then an outlandishly-clad character, a hillbilly version of the village idiot, began clowning with the audience and with the leader of the band, a musician named Mike. Mike's pretty blond wife Dale was the singer in the band. She looked like Rosemary Clooney.

The pace quickened. White gospel turned black, and rousing. The village idiot picked up a pair of drumsticks, and displayed hidden talents as he joined the band. The musicians moved from gospel, to rock, to bluegrass, to blues, and on to Christmas standards. I held my breath as one of the band members, a musician named Steve Bush, launched into a solo. His playing and his picking were sublime. In startling staccato his fingers flew over a bluegrass banjo, and coaxed melancholy melody out of a mandolin. This was one tight band. They took obvious pleasure in each other's company, as comfortable and playful as a family clan. They also teased and joshed the audience. Mike roared out the names of neighbouring states. "Anyone from Alabama?"

"Yes!"

"From Tennessee?"

"Here!"

"Are there folks from Missouri!"

"Right here!"

"From Kansas?" Bo announced her presence. When Mike thought he had all accounted for I piped up.

"You forgot Canada!"

The master of ceremonies swivelled his head. "Did someone say they were from Canada?!"

I was getting into the spirit of jamboree. "I did!"

Mike did a double take. The back-up group grinned.

"Well!" The lady from Canada was seated next to the lady from Kansas. "You gals travellin' together?"

The gal from Canada and the gal from Kansas nodded in assent. It seemed as if every head in the audience had turned to inspect me. The MC consulted with the village idiot.

"A visitor all the way from Canada! This is a special occasion. We ought to do something about this!"

"Yuk! Yuk!" The village idiot agreed. Mike and The Idiot Character leered at each other in conspiracy. After a pregnant pause, Mike turned to the audience and announced, "Because this young (sic) lady has come all the way from Canada, we have a special gift for her and for her companion. For the two ladies we will be giving away – dinner for two!" The audience gasped. Bo perked up. The hillbilly idiot came dashing up the aisle. Stepping on the toes of people seated next to us, he leaned over and tossed into my arms – a boxed Kraft macaroni and cheese dinner.

The audience roared. Bo hid her disappointment. The hillbilly idiot flapped back onstage, beaming at the MC. Mike patted the top of The Idiot Character's red cap and, satisfied that he had done good, The Idiot Character returned to the bandstand and once more metamorphosed from silly clown into serious musician.

In honour of upcoming Veterans' Day, Dale did a turn as all three Andrew Sisters, and Mike launched into an original ballad about a soldier in Iraq. The song was defensive and defiant. The American states don't seem united so much as strung together. They sustain so many different and diametrically-opposed cultures, it's a wonder they've engaged in only one civil war.

There were two intermissions, during which the musicians mingled with the audience. Audience members approached to examine the exotic bird that had flown from so far up north. Steve Bush told me about the two years he spent working as a ranch hand in Alberta, and explained the history of the hoedown, bluegrass music, and the jamboree. I bought one of his CDs, and let him know it. When the show recommenced I waved the disc over my head, so he could see. Back home, in the harsh winter to come, I would listen to Steve Bush's bluegrass banjo while outside my window, another blizzard whited out my world.

Having started my professional life on the stage, I understood the current connecting performer and audience. The musicians were hungry for feedback and eager to please. This show was billed as a holiday show. It ran almost three hours. These hardworking performers would give of themselves in this fashion almost every evening into early December. In the New Year, they would go on tour.

Out in the cold November night, I half-danced to the car. Back in my romantic room I lay on the bed fit-for-a-queen, nibbling my way through a second box of too-salty popcorn. Perhaps the spirits of visitors past were hovering in the rock walls.

The next day, at high noon, me and Bo rode out of the mountain-world.

WINTER, 2008

GOING HOLLYWOOD

We stepped out of a limousine donated by the town's funeral home. We stepped onto the red carpet donated by the town hospital. The searchlights, donated by McDonald's and set up on a residential balcony adjacent to the town's one theatre used for stage shows and live events, was not yet in operation because it was still daylight.

My mother and I were in Fort Scott, Kansas, for the world premiere of a Hallmark Hall of Fame production. Having a connection to the story, and having served as an unofficial consultant to the writer/director, my mother was guest of honour. I was flown in with her, as a kind of *aide-de-camp*. As we made our entrance, one of Mum's arms linked with mine, the other, gripping the handle of a cane, we were confronted by the local paparazzi. A slew of digital cameras snapped at us like the jaws of baby crocodiles. Our image would be published on the front page of the *Fort Scott Tribune* the next day.

The Liberty Theatre was built in the 1880s and has been repeatedly renovated. On the *parterre*, special attendees were seated at round tables. John Kent Harrison, the writer/director of the film, looking far more relaxed than he had in Hollywood two nights before, sat down next to me before noticing that his name was written on a card on a table behind us, together with a group of Hallmark executives. "Oh no, I have to go and sit there." Throughout the screening of the film I would feel Harrison's eyes on my back, as he watched me watching his film. At the private screening for 500 on the lot of the old Twenty-Century Fox studio, he sat three rows behind me and my mother. When my mother was introduced and called to the stage, I stood with her. In early winter, an injury rendered Mum disabled. She was shut in, shuffling with the aid of a walker. Only a month before this event she began intensive chiropractic treatment. I had told her that by the evening of the Hollywood premiere, she would walk down the aisle of the Zanuck Theatre holding my arm with one hand, and sporting a cane on the other. As we rose, suddenly Mum brushed me aside. "I'm going by myself!" My mother began her descent down an inclined aisle. I walked several steps behind her, like a parent anxiously guarding as its child crosses the street for the first time. The audience noticed. "Who is that elegant woman?" Someone whispered. Down front, one of the young Kansans, seeing me hover, leapt up, raced to my mother, and escorted her onto the stage.

At six pm we were picked up by limousine in the boutique hotel Hallmark was housing us in, and driven to the Fox studio. With the aid of a walker, Mum moved down the long city-like blocks of the studio lot, while I carried her cane. As we approached the entrance of the Zanuck Theatre, we noticed a set of stairs. While I wondered how my Mum would negotiate them, a moving platform rolled in front of us, and its driver instructed us to climb aboard. The movie stars took the stairs. We floated above the stars; Mummy, her walker, her cane, and me.

It was in the dead of winter that my mother first received a call from John Kent Harrison. He was steered to her by a woman in Warsaw, who has become my mother's best friend. He had been hired by Hallmark to write and direct a film about the Polish wartime heroine Irena Sendler, who died in May of 2007, at the age of ninety-eight. By profession a social worker, Sendler led a team which rescued 2500 Jewish children from the Warsaw Ghetto. My mother's friend Bieta was a six-month-old infant when she was smuggled out of the Ghetto in a box cut with air holes on its sides. Her parents placed a silver spoon in the box alongside the baby with the engraved inscription, "Elizabeth, January 5, 1942". Bieta refers to the spoon as her birth certificate. Bieta was raised Catholic by a colleague of Sendler's, and took care of her rescuer until the day Sendler died.

The Montreal branch of The Association of Children of The Holocaust was born in my mother's living room. I had brought home a McGill University professor, born in Amsterdam in 1938, on the same street where the German refugee family Frank lived, along with their daughter Anne. At the time, the two of us were roaming around with tape recorders in hand; recording interviews; capturing memories. When Yehudi set up an oral history program at McGill, my mother joined him as co-interviewer. It was in her capacity as a Holocaust educator that my mother met Bieta in Warsaw, which ultimately led to an introduction to Sendler. My mother would discover that her repeated rescues were facilitated by members of Sendler's team. She was with Sendler in Warsaw when the old woman, crippled by her torture at the hands of the Germans, received word that a group of American teenagers were about to call on her. They sent her a letter in February, 2000, and she had wrote back.

"I have no idea what this is about. You'd better stick around," Sendler instructed my mother. "You speak English."

Four high school girls from the hamlet of Uniontown, in Kansas, discovered the identity of Sendler while researching material for a high school history project. They wrote and performed a short play about her wartime exploits, and with this play would tour North America for the next ten years. They also presented the play in Poland. Their teacher won both state and national awards.

The iconic Hallmark Hall of Fame film production company was located ninety miles away, in Kansas City. The daughter of Hallmark's owner attended a performance of *Life in a Jar* and excitedly told her father about it, but no action was taken until several years later, when an independent producer bought the rights to Sendler's story and approached the television film giant. It was only then that the internationally established Hallmark contacted a writer/director who had worked for them in the past. In Divine alignment John Kent Harrison, while filming in Poland, had been given Sendler's biography and was smitten by the tale of this diminutive, indomitable wartime heroine.

In Warsaw, in winter, Bieta told the Hallmark producers and Harrison, "I was just a baby; I don't remember anything. There's a woman in Montreal you should be speaking to. She's my best friend. She's older. She remembers everything."

"How old is this woman?"

"She's 80."

Harrison was sceptical. According to Bieta, he appeared to doubt whether a woman of such an advanced age would have retained her marbles, but he contacted my mother anyway. Mum has a lethal memory. So do I. Often, it feels like a curse.

The writer/director sent Mum a Polish version of his first draft. Her reaction was swift, and succinct. She tossed the script on her dining room table.

"This is not the way it happened! This is nonsense!"

Mum has never been wishy-washy. I smiled.

"You know, Ma, if you were in my writing workshop, you'd have to find another way of saying that."

"Oh yeah? Like how?"

"Well, how about, 'The script doesn't tell the real story.'"

"Hmmph. Maybe I'll ask to see an English version. They're making this movie in English. Why would I want to read it in Polish? I'm in Canada sixty years! Like I didn't have time to learn English?!"

Upon request, Mum received and studied the English version. Again, the verdict was rendered. "This isn't much better."

"Well Ma, it seems you're in a position where you can help the writer improve his script." Guarding sacred memories, my defensive mother didn't recognize the opportunity at hand.

"Aw, you remember what happened with that other script I was asked to help with! They turned it into a travesty! I worked with those people and they did what they wanted anyway! They offered to put my name on the screen in the credits. I told them, 'If you dare put my name on that piece of trash I'll sue you!' And they were Jews! This guy is a *goy* from Ontario. I looked him up on the internet! They gave him this movie to make because the last movie he did was about the Pope! A Polish Pope; a Polish heroine – close enough! How could he possibly understand the Warsaw Ghetto! And Hallmark is producing it! Hallmark?! Achhh! They'll turn it into syrup!" I understood my mother's fears.

"He's a writer, Ma, and you're a resource. If he has integrity, if he cares about what he's doing, he'll be smart enough to listen to you. And you know," I warned my traumatized mama, "this movie will be made whether you participate or not, so you may as well get involved. You can only help to make it better. Besides," I reminded this fierce, formidable, profoundly damaged woman, "it's your duty. You owe it to Sendler's memory." Finally, she was convinced. Thus began what would develop into a special working relationship between two people who would not meet face-to-face until the film's Hollywood premiere; a relationship which would grow into feelings of mutual affection and respect.

I spent a lot of time with my mother that winter. Often, I was on the premises when Harrison called from his cell phone on location in Latvia, to consult with Mum on a detail. It was a good sign.

I've always been uncomfortable attending the premieres of Holocaust-related films; so much so that I stopped attending them. I felt embarrassed getting dolled up to watch the suffering and starvation of children in rags, and then being part of an audience feasting at a buffet. Sitting in Hollywood beside my mother, with the tense, perspiring Harrison seated three rows behind us, I shed my discomfort and lost my embarrassment. The film works, and both Harrison and I know his film is as good as it is because of my mother's contribution to it.

The day before we left for Los Angeles, while I was busy with last-minute packing, my mother called. "I have a favour to ask you." Coming from my mother, a request is considered a command. "They're probably going to ask me to give a speech. They usually do, at these sorts of things. I've written something, and I want you to read it."

At first, I thought Mum was asking me to proofread and edit her speech. It turned out to be more than that.

"I'm going to be too emotional to deliver it. I want you to read it for me."

"You want me to stand on a stage in front of 500 invited guests in Hollywood and deliver a speech in your name?"

"Yes."

My mother is a Holocaust star; she knows how to deliver a speech. "What are you up to, Ma?"

"I want Hollywood to see what a gorgeous daughter I have. I want to see you back in the limelight." Mum was referring to the fact that I began my professional life on the stage.

The prospect was tempting; it was also terrifying. I worked on my mother's speech, and then, in a moment of panic, e-mailed the Hallmark representative I had been in touch with while making travel arrangements, and asked her if a speech was expected.

"No. We're all going to just sit back and enjoy the moment."

When the moment came, my mother was asked to "Please say a few words." Mum demurred. She's the greatest actress I've ever known. Her performance was so pitch perfect that it almost convinced me.

At the reception, one of the Hallmark executives lauded her decision to remain silent. "You were right. Always leave 'em wanting more."

Mum eyed me ruefully, hissing, "Do you feel as frustrated as I do?"

"Yes and no. I may have missed the moment, but it just didn't feel right. It's Harrison's night."

At the reception I entered into a long conversation with Harrison's assistant editor. I confessed my dilemma.

"Oh! I'm so sorry you didn't! I would've loved to have heard the speech! I would've listened to you and seen you as a conduit for your mother. Even a truncated version would be worth listening to. Perhaps you can cobble together something for the premiere on Wednesday night. And hey, this is Hollywood. Everyone's looking out for their next job. There's nothing wrong with being ambitious and wanting to shine."

I was staggered by audience reaction to my mother. At the reception, actors and screenwriters and directors and producers insisted on paying homage to her for no other reason, but that she had survived. The real heroine is dead, and Mum was an accessible piece of living history connected to her. *(2024: I cringe upon reading this line. I had internalized my mother's opinion of herself as being "no one and nothing special caught in a killing machine". To be among the category of less than one per cent of children under the age of fifteen who not only survived the infamous Warsaw Ghetto, but went on to survive the rest of the war was, of course, heroic.)*

As Mum perched on the seat of her walker, Hollywood luminaries moved in. "Tell me your story! I want to shake your hand!" Some just observed, as if Mum were a relic on exhibit in a museum. I recognized one of them. She is a mature, aging woman now; still classy, still attractive. She stood apart, silently contemplating my mother. Fifty years ago, she incarnated Margot Frank in one of the first films dealing with the *Shoah*. Forty years ago, she played Maximilian Schell's love interest in an adventure epic. I remembered watching it on television and mulling on how lovely she was. I remembered musing how I'd like to look like her. Now here we were at a reception on the lot of the studio where she began her career, our shoulders draped in glittering shawls, in concession to the cool California evening. She, a seventy-one-year-old film producer whose once-raven hair is highlighted an artificial gold, me, an obscure fifty-three-year-old writer from Canada whose chestnut-coloured hair is streaked a God-given silver. On what was she reflecting as she regarded Hallmark's poster child for the Holocaust? Was she remembering Otto Frank, who wept when he met the dark, wholesome beauty who bore such a startling resemblance to his dead daughter Margot? As she stared at my mother in the midst of *Shoah* business, she caught me staring at her. "Are you Diane Baker?"

"Yes, I am." An infinitesimal lift of an eyebrow betrayed her surprise at being recognized. Her close-mouthed smile mirrored mine. What else could I say? There was nothing more to say. All I could do was savour the moment.

When Mum and I returned to our executive suite, we went to work on reconstructing the speech. Just before two am, when I could do no more, she found a copy of what she'd originally written, tucked away in her suitcase.

We left the smog-choked Hollywood hills at nine the next morning, for an eleven am flight to Kansas City. We were traveling with the executives from Hallmark, and with the troupe from Fort Scott. The four high school girls who created the original production of *Life in a Jar* are young married women now. As an airport official snaked my mother's wheelchair through a serpentine route in Los Angeles' massive airport; we followed behind like ducks in a row: the Hallmark executives, me, and the young women, with one of their husbands in tow. I had negotiated a Business Class ticket for my mother on the Montreal-Los Angeles flight, but now we were all flying Economy. On a midget airline called *Midwest*, we even had to pay to check in our bags. *(2024: In 2009, this was unheard of.)* As we scrunched into the cramped seats, Mama Duck turned to one of the Hallmark executives and quacked, "I'd think you guys would have private jets!"

"We do," he admitted. "But we're not using them this year." I would later learn that Hallmark is in the process of laying off 750 employees. Those who manage to hold onto their jobs are grateful to be traveling with the masses.

From the Emerald City, we were airlifted to Kansas. We arrived in The Heartland along with spring. Tender primavera leaves peaked through their buds. The air was dry and crystalline. Farm lands shimmered under wide prairie skies. Shadows fell disconcertingly early, because we lost two of the three hours we'd gained on going to California. Our arrival in Kansas was a kind of homecoming for me, as well as for my companions. Eighteen months earlier, I spent several weeks on a ranch outside Fort Scott as the guest of a woman who was one of the chaperones on the Kansas troupe's visit to Poland. I never imagined I would be transported back so soon.

We reached Fort Scott after six pm. Main Street was deserted, except for the warm, welcoming presence of Norman Conard. Norman is a multiple-award-winning educator who was the inspiration and catalyst for the high school history project which rescued the legacy of the rescuer Sendler. No longer in the classroom, he is now the director of The Lowell

Milken Education Center in Fort Scott. While his former students, founders of the *Life in a Jar* project, travelled to California, Norman remained in town to finalize arrangements for the premiere, and for our stay. I had met him several times, briefly and on the fly, but it would be on this trip, for the next two days, that I discovered why his protégées, as well as my mother, adore him.

It was Norman who arranged for the two limousines, the red carpet, the klieg lights, and the theatre. Creative, dynamic, and surprisingly sweet, the beloved "Mr. Conard" is a middle-aged Andy Hardy who involved the whole town in putting on a show. While it hosted the world premiere of a film, Fort Scott's spirit was reminiscent of Frank Capra's cinematic American towns. Hollywood fever had hit the Midwest, and its inhabitants seemed high on helium.

During our stay in Fort Scott my mother and I were housed in The Pink Cottage across the street from The Big House. The Big House is one of twin Victorian mansions operated by the Lyons family as a guest house. Harrison and the Hallmark executives were housed in The Big House, while Mum and I were sheltered in a dream cottage, which we had to ourselves. We assumed Hallmark was sponsoring our stay, just as it had in Hollywood. We would later learn that the use of this romantic abode, built in 1930 and lovingly restored and decorated like a museum, had been donated.

After a day of traveling, Mum and I dropped onto our ergonomically-designed four-poster beds, overwhelmed. Mum said it for us both. "There are hidden treasures in this country."

The anachronistically fresh air of the flatlands knocked out my mother like a drug. I slept-walked through this living dream. A bathroom with black-slate tiles led into a walk-in overhead shower which mimicked a rain shower. It was augmented with strategically-placed horizontal jet streams. Off the bathroom there was a room-sized, soft beige-toned boudoir for milady. The fully-equipped kitchen, its window overlooking a back porch and small garden, had a digital oven and stove top, and under the silent ceiling fan there was a counter bar flanked by leather-covered stools. On the edge of the kitchen counter, as an accent, sat a cowboy-boot-shaped crystal mug. In what might've been a dining room there was a long desk with a globe perched on its edge. The desk was positioned in front of an electric fireplace. In the darkness, against the mahogany panelling I could envision one Samuel Clemens, an extravagantly-moustachioed riverboat captain, dipping a quill into an ink pot and composing another tall tale destined for publication in a newspaper across the state line.

It is "Miss Pat", a glamorous, saucer-eyed grandmother, who watches over The Twins and The Pink like a guest-house goddess. She is assisted by her son Nate, who resembles a younger George Clooney.

"For anything simple, call me," she instructed as she taped phone numbers next to the wall phone. "For anything technical, call Nate."

Miss Pat brought in a dish of fresh fruit salad, yogurt mixed with nutmeg and vanilla, and a baggie-full of homemade granola, studded with walnuts and pecans harvested from a local farm.

"For breakfast, so I won't disturb you in the morning."

Nate presented himself after I sent an S.O.S., when unable to activate the digital oven.

After feeding myself and my drowsy, contented mother with baked potatoes and kefir purchased during a quick stop at *Woods*, I fell into my four-poster. The whistle of the trains broke the stillness of the night. Behind my eyes I could see the statuesque "Harvey Girls" in their long aprons, their cinched shirt-waists, their World War II coifs, their dazzling MGM smiles and their sizzling MGM tans. Echoing through the ether like a lullaby came the voice of the golden-throated Garland crooning, "All the way to Califor-nii—Ayyy on the Atchison, Topeka, and the Santa Fe!"

I turned to the night table. An ornately carved tray rested on its edge. There was a colourful slip of paper inserted into the tray, and in elaborate calligraphy it read, *"It is 1876. Fort Scott is the Rail center of the Frontier, bringing supplies to fledgling mercantiles, loading precious coal, paint, cement and flagstone, and heading WEST! Thus began the romance that exists today between Fort Scott's citizens and the railroads. We locals consider the long whines and whistles from the Burlington-Northern music to our ears. If you are not quite as enamoured, here are earplugs to ensure your uninterrupted night."* Miss Pat thought of everything.

Oh! What a beautiful morning! Oh! What a beautiful day! Wednesday, April 15 glowed in living Technicolor. No one locks their doors in CapraLand. Before we had time to realize we needed something, a friendly soul would poke her face through the door, and just happen to be able to supply it.

In a phone call to the Milken Center, I informed Megan that Mum was prepared to give the speech she'd refused to give on Monday evening in Hollywood. A few moments later, the wall next to the Mark Twainish desk vibrated, as the phone rang.

"Ahh, Brent said there won't be time for speeches, so you don't have to bother. You can relax." I was hearing echoes.

"Ma, who was it who asked you to give a speech on Monday night?"

"Brent."

"That doesn't make sense."

"Then maybe it was Brad. I get those COEs mixed up."

"CEOs. And there's only one of them."
"What?"
I sighed." "Never mind."

Brad was the president of Hallmark; Brent was the producer of the film. Tweedledee was saying yes; Tweedledum was saying no.

Mum and I looked at each other in consternation. *Fool me once, shame on you; fool me twice...* At the same instant, we reached the same conclusion. "Get it ready. Prepare the speech."

Mum was trundled off for another round of media interviews. Hallmark was getting its money's worth. As the self-styled *aide-de-camp*, I had little more to do than enjoy the almost impossibly perfect day. I took my notebook, the speech, and several miniature red mugs filled with mint tea onto the back porch. There was a small running fountain on the porch. A fully-stocked fish pond nestled underneath. The enclosed yard contained patio furniture, a grill, and a fire pit. All was sheltered by an old oak tree.

I sat in the sun, editing my mother's speech. Despite what I had told Megan, I expected to be delivering it that evening. When I was done I luxuriated in the private rain shower, stretched on a rug in front of the electric fireplace, and then took the speech across the street to The Big House, to type it up on Miss Pat's computer. On the steps of the Lyons mansion, a photographer was taking pictures of a family of children. I took a few moments to swing on the front porch swing, like a frontier gal waitin' for her fella to come a callin'. I borrowed a 1948 edition of *Life* magazine, which lay on the coffee table in the front parlour. After placing it on the quilted spread of my mother's four-poster, I took a stroll along the shady, tree-lined streets of this sparkling Caprasque town.

At the cocktail hour, one of two limousines drove up to the

entrance of the cottage. (The other drove back and forth from The Big House, chauffeuring Harrison and the group from Hallmark.) The driver emerged, and waited on the sidewalk. Becky Halsey and her husband came to the door to fetch us. Becky Halsey, henceforth to be referred to as "Jelloshot Becky", had designated herself our official escort for the evening. She told Norman as much. She insisted upon it.

A showdown between Jelloshot Becky and Mama took place at the turn of this century, when my mother was brought to Fort Scott for the first time, as a living example of a rescued child: an added attraction to the *Life in a Jar* student play. Norman held a party in his home. Becky was one of the guests. Like many Midwesterners, she bubbles with friendliness and hospitality. What the townsfolk knew, and Mum did not, is that Becky's culinary speciality is Jell-O Shots. Jell-O Shots are cubes of Jell-O laced with vodka. Bubbly Becky approached the stranger aiming a tray upon which was balanced slippery red gelatinous cubes.

"Jell-O SHAT!" She eyeballed my mother. Becky knew the older woman had been born in Europe. "Jell-O SHAT!" She nodded emphatically, raising a spoon.

Instantly, my cosmopolitan mother understood what she was dealing with. Mischievously, she widened her eyes and slowly, hesitantly repeated, "Jeeellow SHAAAWT!"

"Very good!" Becky was pleased with how quickly the foreigner was learning. She dropped a cube down her gullet, handed my mother one of the spoons lying on the tray, and motioned to her to do the same. Gleefully, Mum played her part. She picked up a spoon and scooped up a cube. She batted the eyelashes shading her steely blue-grey peepers. Becky missed the glint in them.

"Jello SHAWT?"

Becky was impressed. "Yes! Yes! Jello SHAT!'" Becky made the rounds of the room, and kept circling back to Mum.

"Jello Shat!" She coached her protégée. "Jello Shat!" Mute, Mum would nod, and scoop up another cube. This pattern continued for several rounds. The Pole in my mother is familiar with the effects of vodka. When she began to feel them she erupted, "Goddamit! What the hell's going on here?! Norman!" Mama wailed across the room. "This woman is getting me drunk!" Becky reeled. So did my mama, but for a different reason. The joke was on both of them.

Now Becky, her husband and the senior partner of the funeral home brought us to a wine and cheese reception at the Milken Center on Main Street. I wound my way to the back of the crowded office, where the fruit and water was located. In the small, tight space I knocked against the back of a gentleman, and we turned to face each other. His small round eyes flashed, and his big round face broke into a wide, delighted smile. It was John Kent Harrison. We hadn't seen each other since the premiere in Hollywood, two nights before. To my surprise, the director of the film flung his arms around me. On this soft spring evening, he was expansive and relaxed. After a year of intense, focused labour, Harrison knew he'd birthed a success.

Though the Liberty Theatre was one block down on the other side of the street, we V.I.P.s-for-the-evening were bustled back into the limousine and driven around the corner and beyond in order to make the ride look longer. Our chauffeur was the father of a father-and-son-run funeral home, a white-haired gentleman by the name of Jerry Witt. Indeed.

In front of the theatre, Mercy Hospital's red carpet had been slung onto the sidewalk like a scarlet bolt laid out on display in a material shop. Mum and I were startled by the sight of townsfolk and local paparazzi lined up on the pavement; their cameras aimed and ready to shoot. We stared at the crowd, at each other, and then grinned in conspiracy. Our chauffeur stopped, emerged, and opened the back doors. I stepped out. My amber earrings danced as I slung my lime-coloured scarf across a shoulder of my emerald fake fur jacket, clutched my shimmering chocolate-coloured, egg-shaped evening bag in one hand, and offered my free arm to my Mum. We strolled down the scarlet bolt, deigning to the crowd. One of many pictures snapped at that moment would appear on the front page of the *Fort Scott Tribune* the next morning. When I saw it, I screamed with laughter. My glee turned bittersweet when I noticed the date at the top of the page: April 16 is my father's birthday. One doesn't need a passport to come from The Other Side. But of course his blithe spirit would hover over such an event, watching over his two stars.

In the photograph I am smiling sweetly, and move with my head held high. Mum is wielding her cane and leering at the camera, those steely blue-greys proclaiming, "Bring it on!" This same photograph would later be placed on Hallmark's website.

As we passed the buffet laid out in the outdoor courtyard at the back entrance to the theatre, our escort Becky offered me a drink.

"I wouldn't accept anything from you which wasn't labelled and sealed," I deadpanned. Becky blinked, and then handed me a bottle of *Ozarka* spring water.

Inside the theatre, my mother was corralled for yet another interview; this time, with NBC. I marvelled at how skilfully and relentlessly Mum steered clear of personal questions, and repeatedly focused the limelight on the subject at hand.

After Harrison reluctantly vacated the seat next to me in order to sit with Tweedledee and Tweedledum, the spot was filled by the ubiquitous Becky. As the lights dimmed and the film unfolded, her cheerful visage turned dark with distress. Tears tumbled into sobs which cascaded into waterfalls of weeping as the misery and horror of the story took hold. By the time the film ended, our little round table was studded with balled-up wads of tissue. I was seeing the film for the second time. As my mother's daughter, I was infinitely better prepared for the material than Becky, but still there were moments when I looked away from images too harrowing to confront head on and when I did, its creator leaned over to stroke my back.

"It's even better the second time," I whispered. When the film ended and the houselights switched on, I signalled Harrison and pointed to the bouquet of tissues on our table. One writer smiled ruefully at the other. Becky was a quivering wreck. It was a supreme compliment to the film's creator.

After preliminary speeches on stage, Tweedledee announced, "I have known Renata for only two days, but in that time I have learnt that this spunky lady will do what she wants to do, and will not do what she doesn't want to do. And so, I ask that she say a few words. Please." The president of Hallmark almost pleaded. This time, we were ready. I expected to receive the speech from my mother's hand and deliver it for her, but as I rose from my seat she hissed, "No! I have to do this myself!" Leaning on the cane, she ambled her way to the stage. Norman called, "Sharon! Help your mother!" Well, really.

I stood off to the side while Mum delivered her speech; then helped her off the stage. We were re-called for group photographs. As I stood on the stage I heard a voice both strange and strangely familiar, calling from out of the darkness.

"Sharon."

I looked down, into the audience area. There stood a woman I knew, yet barely recognized. It was, and wasn't Bo. In the eighteen months since I'd left, the isolated ranch wife, seemingly trapped, had shed half of the 100 extra pounds she'd buried herself in, as well as the cunning, handsome husband of forty-two years whose leaving was saving her life. She had let her hair grow out, and was allowing it to retain its natural colour. The angles of her face, previously distorted by obesity, were visible again. So was Bo's natural sweetness. My stay on her ranch, though quiet, was not always peaceful. For separate reasons, my presence proved disturbing to both husband and wife. I left saddened, believing the next time I would receive news of her would be to hear of her passing.

"Bonnie!" I dashed down the side steps of the stage, towards my old friend. "I was on the lookout for you when I came in. You must've been sitting upstairs (in the balcony). I figured you would find me."

Bo was suffering, yet energized by anger. "The land alone is worth a million. When I know what the settlement is, I'll move to the other side of the state, near my daughter, and build myself a home with a clubhouse and a pool!"

"A swimming pool? You wouldn't go swimming with me." As the words fell from my mouth, I understood. "If I can swim – where no one can see me – then I would do it." I knew exactly what she meant. As a teenager, I swam off seventy pounds in the privacy of an indoor apartment pool.

"Come outside. Let's take a walk." This, from a woman who would find every excuse not to walk. I want to show you my new car!" Bo and I walked into the courtyard, where a post-film reception was in full swing. She walked past tables heaped with food, seemingly blind to them. I remembered when she was compulsively chomping on items edible and barely so, as if doing so helped her to breathe.

On the sidewalk, on Main Street nearing midnight, I waved as Bo rode off. "You go, Girl," I said softly. It was meant for both of us.

I returned to the courtyard, where my mother sat with Harrison and several others. He broke the fourth wall and told tales of what went on behind the scenes during the film's production.

Most of the capacity 575-member audience had left. For the few diehards – and me, who had no choice – Becky produced a large ceramic bowl containing her gleaming red specialty, which had spent the evening in the theatre's cooling storage unit. Becky needed it. Harrison had earned it.

Along with the bowl, Becky whipped out a set of silver soup spoons. Harrison had been warned in advance.

"Sharon, have one."

"No thanks. I don't drink."

The diehards gathered around the bowl for another group photograph. All, including the director, raised their spoons, posed, and smiled for the camera.

Becky and her husband accompanied us as the junior Witt drove us back to the pink cottage. Becky was bleary-eyed, yet requested a tour of the cottage. My mother, who is not only the life of every party but also its afterlife, was happy to oblige.

Becky stumbled around the cottage like a drowsy child resisting sleep. At one thirty in the morning, I suggested the Halseys go home. Relieved, they complied. My mother is never more chipper than in the wee hours after a party. The trains whistled and Mum chirped. At three am, I handed her the 1948 edition of *Life* magazine, and retired to my four-poster in the room next to hers.

Norman came to the back porch at eleven the next morning. Mum was up. "I didn't want to come too early."

"Oh, no problem! Sharon!"

I quashed one of the large, marshmallowy pillows over my head.

"No no! Let her sleep!" Norman's protectiveness was

reminiscent of my dad's. My dad... as I came to consciousness on the late morning of April 16, I remembered the significance of the date. Daddy had died on April 6, was buried on April 10, and born on April 16. Each year during that ten-day span, he sends a gift of some kind. This year, Daddy outdid himself.

I rose at noon and took a last, long April shower. Before three in the afternoon Norman, Mum and I hit the road for the outskirts of Kansas City. We would be staying at the airport hotel overnight, and flying home the next day. Norman would spend the night near the airport, too. He would be flying out to Los Angeles for a conference. Norman would be staying at a Comfort Inn; we would be staying at the Hyatt. Our night at the Hyatt was covered by a private donation.

Halfway between Fort Scott and Kansas City I noticed a sign I would never see at home; *Massacre Site 5 m*. I assumed it was connected to the Civil War. The sighting of the sign elicited an enlightening, informative lecture from our driver/host/history teacher, and a list of recommended reading which would feed my literary appetite for months to come. We had gone to America to honour the history my mother emerged from, and I came home with a heightened interest in American history.

We took a late lunch break at a roadside cafeteria called *Dean and Deluca*. Mindful of my culinary experience during my first trip to the Midwest, Norman wanted to show me that not all Kansans would fry their children, if it were legal.

At *Dean and Deluca*, one walks with a tray from counter to counter, and makes one's selections. The woman behind the bread counter recognized Norman. She was a Jewish woman of my generation. She had just lost her father, who was a Holocaust survivor. Norman told her who we were, and why we had come. Excitedly she rushed over to greet Mummy.

The name tag attached to the young man behind the vegetable counter read "Adam", which is my nephew's name, and the name my mother called my father because she didn't like the name "Abram". I had been running on adrenalin for five days; now fatigue was setting in. I dropped a bottle of water. The bottle was made of glass. The young man carrying the name of my father and my father's namesake came over with a broom and a smile. As he swept up the broken shards Adam proclaimed, *"Mazel Tov!"* My water was replaced, and we raised our glasses in a toast to a ghost.

Norman had booked us on the first floor at the Hyatt in order to spare my mother unnecessary movement. In the hotel room, he wrote down his contact numbers before retiring to the Inn. Like Miss Pat, Norman, too, thought of everything. For a half day I felt cradled by a warm, protective male presence. Into early adulthood I took this feeling for granted. When I lost my father, I lost my buffer against a harsh world. Now, for a half day on his birthday, once again, briefly, I felt safe.

Yet I knew I was safe. I knew we would all be safe; me, my mum, Bonnie – all the courageous-hearted women who would, and will rescue themselves.

SPRING AND SUMMER, 2009

BENE MERITO: THE STORY OF EWA JANINA WOCJICKA

A dwarf from the slums of Warsaw who rose to heroic stature in wartime

At the end of June 2011, Mum, Michael and I received the news that her cancer had resurfaced and this time, it was inoperable. Mum's battle with cancer had lasted longer than the war, and it appeared she was about to lose it. Still, my brother Michael insisted that she proceed with plans for a trip to Poland. Michael promised to accompany her. Michael is a medical doctor, and his repeated interventions repeatedly extended our mother's life. Renata would be safe with her son.

In Warsaw, at summer's end, a conference was going to be held by a network of world Jewry whose members survived the Holocaust as children. It would be the twentieth anniversary of a group known as *The Association of Children of The Holocaust.* For ten of those twenty years Renata worked to have a conference held in Warsaw. Her dream was coming true. Her nightmare was unending.

Treatment was started, and Michael fulfilled his promise to accompany Mum to Poland. The day before the conference, Mum was invited to a reception held by the Polish government's foreign ministry, where an outstanding schoolteacher was to receive an award as Best Teacher of the Year for Holocaust Studies. As Mum sat in the audience beside her son, her name was called. She was instructed to approach the podium. In a daze, she struggled to her feet. Despite the air-conditioning, her auburn-coloured wig itched. The eighty-two-year-old cancer patient limped to the front of the hall with the aid of a cane. She supported herself, standing on her feet, while a representative of the foreign ministry read out a list of her achievements, and bestowed upon her a medal for the Order of Merit.

A hall filled with a hundred people; teachers and their families, government officials, diplomats, and a rabbi, leapt to their feet, applauding in ovation. Michael remained in his seat. He was stunned.

Mum was confused. Through her partial deafness, she managed to decipher that she was receiving this award for her part in having her wartime Polish rescuers honoured as Righteous Gentiles, and for her ceaseless activism in building bridges of understanding and forgiveness between Polish Catholics and Polish Jews.

Still, Mum could not process the meaning of the award. "This can't be for me," she thought, growing haunted. She felt tugged by the memory of a doll-like young woman, perfectly formed, who seemed to have been created in miniature. She was so petite that those who knew her called her "Lilliput". She had a wide and open face, wore her ash blonde hair in a straight and flat pageboy, dressed in children's clothes because they came in the only size that fit, and wrapped her slender torso in an ornately patterned peasant's shawl. She hovered in Mum's heart and mind for seven decades, refusing to leave. Perceiving her own approaching end, Mum feared the story and memory of the woman she considered her surrogate mother would die with her. "This isn't for me." Mum was already distanced from the proceedings of the present, and slipped into the parallel universe of her past. "This award," she told herself. "No. All of it. My whole life, the lives of my children and my grandchildren, all of it, I owe to my Janka."

Ewa Janina Wojcicka was born in the slums of Warsaw on Christmas Eve of 1908. She was the daughter of labourers. She had an older sister. She had been in Natalia's employ since she was a teenager. Family interference tore apart Natalia's marriage, and she and her husband separated in 1935.

For the beleaguered Natalia it would be her housekeeper Janina, known as Janka, who became her lifelong confidante and companion. While Natalia went into the wider world to provide for her children, it was Janka who pushed Renata's perambulator in the Saski Gardens, it was Janka who spoon-fed her kefir, and it was Janka who made her laugh and dried her tears.

For Janka, perhaps Renata filled the space left by the child she was forced to deny. A little girl wove in and out of Natalia's household, born the same year as Renata. She was introduced as Janka's niece. Janka's sister raised her. In fact, the girl was Janka's daughter, the issue of a rape by her bestial brother-in-law.

In the last spring of peace, Janka was once more large and swollen with child. She had spent Christmas with those who passed for family and in the New Year returned to Natalia's apartment carrying another issue of another rape. In the summer Alek, Natalia's son, and her eldest, took Janka for daily walks until he was mobilized into the reserves, and then the two women disappeared into the countryside. When they returned, Janka's silhouette was slim once more.

Renata was slated to resume school in September. September came, but school didn't start. What started in September was the Second World War. When the month-long siege of Warsaw ended and schools re-opened in October under German occupation, only Catholic children were allowed to attend. Renata spent school hours inside the family apartment, reading works of literature Natalia acquired for her from local libraries, while she and her older daughter Ania braved the daily line-ups for bread. Only bakeries were allowed to re-open, under the supervision of the Germans. As they patrolled these line-ups, German soldiers brutalized anyone they suspected of being Jewish. They were assisted in identifying their victims by Polish collaborators who, at this early stage, were mostly teen-age hoodlums heedless of the consequences.

It was an inefficient way of removing the Jews, and the Germans prided themselves on their efficiency. In late autumn posters plastered across the city and news announcements over Polish radio declared that, as of December 1, all Jews over the age of twelve were obliged to wear white armbands illustrated with a blue Star of David. That is when Natalia announced, "We're getting out of here."

While Natalia and Ania spent the days acquiring bread, Janka developed business contacts. Semi-literate, she kept her salary hidden under her mattress. As Natalia's resources dwindled, Janka handed her employer money, as needed. With her seed money Janka began buying from the desperate Jews, and selling to savvy farmers. Even savvier, Janka bartered with the farmers, and pocketed her profits from the Jews. Quickly establishing a reputation as a black market racketeer, Janka used her increasing wealth to keep her adopted family alive. She brought in coal to heat the apartment for the coming winter, along with hefty sacks of potatoes and flour, while Natalia planned the escape of her daughters and then, her own. In the meantime Alek had defected from the defeated Polish army, ditched his uniform, stole a horse and, acquiring clothes from a peasant in a manner that can only be guessed at, rode back into Warsaw, to his mother's house. Natalia then decided that her swarthy, circumcised son must leave first.

On December 1, 1939, Ania and Renata crossed over into Bialystok. Local farmers, who found a new source of income in leading Jews across the border into the Soviet sector, extorted more money from Ania than had been agreed on. Natalia and Janka took the precaution of equipping Ania for such an event and, once the farmers' greed was satisfied, the sisters were able to join Alek in a ramshackle farmhouse on the outskirts of town, filled with fellow refugees.

When Natalia received word that her daughters were safe, she embarked on her own escape. Janka stayed behind in the apartment. It was more wished for, than expected, that the war would be brief, and Natalia and her children would soon return to a home maintained by Janka.

By the time Natalia began her journey in early December of 1939, more and more escape routes were being discovered and sealed. She had to take a roundabout route, and reached Bialystok more than a week after her departure.

Ania, always restless, always reckless, could not endure the wait. She decided to cross back and retrieve her mother. Alek pleaded with her to have patience, and stay put. Generally irrational, Ania could not be reasoned with. She believed she knew the route and did not require the assistance of farmer/smugglers. Going it alone, Ania attempted to re-enter the German zone. She was caught, arrested, beaten and raped. The only reason she survived was because she was able to pass as Catholic. She was allowed to return to her home, only to discover that her mother was no longer there.

By the time she arrived in Bialystok, Natalia was running a fever. A doctor was summoned. Natalia had contracted typhus. She was one of its first victims in the first of many wartime epidemics to come.

Natalia was removed to hospital, not so much for her own sake, but in order to spare the refugee shelter coming under quarantine. There was no medication available. The doctors, and Natalia's children could only watch and wait. The stricken woman survived the disease's first crisis, but succumbed to the second. She died on the first night of the New Year, at the dawn of 1940.

After Natalia was buried, Alek decided that he and Renata must return to Warsaw and be with Ania. Renata was terrified of returning. Alek joined a band of refugees who had decided to go back. Some could not tolerate life in exile. Some could not bear to be separated from their families.

These frightened people were further frightened by the prospect of having a child in their midst. Alek pleaded with them to accept Renata, as he had pleaded with Ania not to attempt a return. The group relented, but Renata did not. Brother and sister had a violent argument. In frustration Alek hit Renata and dragged her to the meeting point. As the adults climbed over and ducked fences, passing a point of no return, Renata made a split-second decision to run. In the other direction. Alek stared in horror at his fleeing sister, but it was too late to turn back. It was not so much the Germans Renata was terrified of returning to; it was Ania.

Without Renata, in Warsaw, it fell to Alek to break the news of Natalia's death to Janka and most traumatically, to Ania. In her frequent fits of hysteria, Ania taunted Alek for "losing the child". Alek finally slipped on the blue and white armband. Doing so would've horrified his mother. Ania continued to defy the order and relied on her ability to pass as Catholic. Despite her dark, slanted eyes and luxuriant dark hair Ania, chameleon-like, could slip out of her Jewish skin and into the persona of a Polish peasant. She could blend and weave in and out of crowds undetected as surely and swiftly as Janka. Together Janka and Ania bought and sold and bartered and bribed, keeping each other and Alek, alive.

On November 15, 1940, under the German occupiers' new law, Ania and Alek were compelled to enter the ghetto established for Jews in Warsaw. On that same date Janka moved out of Natalia's apartment and back into the slums, with her sister and bestial brother-in-law. She arranged to have Natalia's furniture moved to various safe houses, and then began selling it off. With the proceeds, she bought food and smuggled it into the Ghetto, keeping Alek and Ania alive.

After the Germans invaded the Soviet sector in the summer of 1941, Renata was confined to the ghetto established for Jews in Bialystok. On orders from their German masters the local *Judenrat,* the Jewish council, were recruiting young and strong workers to fix potholes on the roads. Renata secured a position in what amounted to a chain gang without chains. Under armed guard, every day in the blistering heat she set out with other incarcerated youngsters, to fix the potholes. They wore yellow patches on their chests and upper backs, as a mark of shame. Each day that their work progressed, they had to walk further to begin it. Each day they passed the Ghetto gates to the taunts and jeers of local Poles, and each evening they re-entered to the sound of the same obscenities. The Jewish children's reward for their slave labour was a small bag of *kasha* handed out at the end of the day, which Renata handed over to the adults who allowed her to share their apartment. Like many Jewish children trapped on a planet gone mad, Renata took a grim pride in keeping adults alive.

One evening, at summer's end, as Renata marched towards the gates of the Ghetto along a gangplank flanked by hate-filled faces and vicious mouths shouting curses she heard, among them, the echo of a familiar voice calling a name only few people knew. "Renusia! Renusia!" It was the diminutive used by family. "Renusia! Renusia!" The voice grew louder and more insistent. Renata, who had learned to avert her gaze from the sight of the nightly mobs, turned to follow the call. A pint-sized woman with luminous blue eyes and a sleek ash blonde pageboy, her tiny torso wrapped in its signature peasant shawl, was calling to her. It was Janka. Renata gaped. Janka slipped through the crowd to Renata's side and with her through the Ghetto gates. Hoping she might find Renata alive, Janka had brought, in a lid-less basket, a five-dollar U.S. bill, in case someone needed to be bribed, a tin medallion engraved with the image of the Virgin Mary, and the Jewish armband worn in Warsaw. The presence of the armband would prove a grievous mistake.

"I came as soon as I could." Janka's understatement was masterful. Renata, stunned and overwhelmed with grief and gratitude, led Janka to the apartment she had access to, where she was allowed to sleep in the hallway. Janka gave another young girl the five-dollar U. S. bill in exchange for two yellow patches and her place in the work detail. She quickly stitched the patches onto the front and back of her blouse, and cradled Renata to sleep in her arms.

At dawn Janka clipped the medallion around Renata's neck, under the nightgown she wore, which doubled as a dress. It was a baby blue-coloured nightgown with a small white flower design, which she belted with a piece of rope during the day. Lining up with a group of Jewish youths as their German captors counted heads, the nanny and her charge marched through the Ghetto gates and onto a hot and dusty road. At noontime, which signalled lunchtime for the German guards and continued work for the Jewish youths, the guards retreated to the shade of trees, enjoying meals brought in on rolling canteens. Satiated and lulled by beer, the German guards grew drowsy. Janka nudged Renata. "Move and keep moving." Gently Janka coaxed Renata into a ditch, dropping down beside her. They crawled on their bellies over the stones and hard grey earth, and then Janka stopped in order to pull the stitches out of the yellow patches on Renata's makeshift dress, and on her own blouse. She wrapped Renata's neck in a kerchief in order to camouflage the holes in the material left by the torn stitches, and then she wrapped her own shoulders in her colourful shawl, to do the same.

When Janka surmised that they had gained sufficient distance, she instructed Renata to rise. Janka was four feet five inches, and twelve-year-old Renata had grown to her full height of five feet four. "Walk slowly. Keep calm." In broad daylight, in blistering heat, the woman-child and the child-woman ambled down country lanes. As they nodded to passing peasants on the road they were hailed with the traditional greeting, "Praise the Lord." Without irony, the Catholic nanny and her Jewish charge responded with the same.

It took Janka and Renata two weeks to reach Warsaw. They sustained themselves by sneaking into barns in the evenings and sleeping there during the nights. Before dawn Janka would wake Renata. They stole eggs from under squatting chickens, cracked their shells, and drank the contents raw. Janka's lid-less basket, covered with a cloth, held a small cup and cans she had picked up along the road. She taught Renata to milk cows and they drank the milk, along with the raw eggs, before the farmers were up and able to catch them at it. On their odyssey to Warsaw, they supplemented their diet from farm fields by stealing carrots and cucumbers and potatoes. They ate the vegetables raw and enjoyed them – even the potatoes.

In downtown Warsaw, Janka and Renata boarded the tramway that ran through the streets of the Ghetto, and back. Police agents patrolled the platforms to make sure that no one dared get on or off until the tramway had returned to the Aryan

Side. Warsaw's transit system was controlled by a socialist union with connections to the Polish underground resistance movement. Should an inmate of the Ghetto manage to board at one end and escape at the other, the drivers would turn a blind eye. Often the drivers tossed loaves of bread out the window, as their route took them through the Ghetto. Sometimes their passengers did the same.

Before boarding the tramway, Janka slipped the armband into Renata's pocket. A sharp curve was coming up on one of the Ghetto streets. The driver would be compelled to slow down. Janka instructed Renata to jump when the driver approached the curve. Renata positioned herself on the back platform, while the patrolling agent spied her from the front. After a summer of hard labour Renata was physically strong and deeply tanned, yet there was tell-tale terror in her eyes. Renata had the look and feel and scent of a hunted animal. The agent was trained to hunt.

Janka caught the agent eyeing his quarry. Her instructions to Renata changed. "Renusia," Janka whispered. "Stay put." She felt they had no choice but to continue riding the tramway full circle and finally, they disembarked at its starting point, on the Aryan Side.

The agent disembarked with them, grabbed Renata, frisked her, and found the armband. He struck her, and declared her under arrest. Renata protested that she had been trying to get into the Ghetto, not out. Though it was true, it was also unbelievable. The agent struck her again, and dragged her off. Janka pleaded with the agent to let the girl go. He shoved Janka out of his way. "You Jewish whore!" The epithet was addressed to Janka. "Stay out of this, or I'll arrest you too!" Helpless, Janka could do no more than watch and follow from a distance.

Renata was taken to a downtown prison and tossed into a cell with a gang of hardened prostitutes. The sight of their

Virgin's image on the body of a Jewish girl enraged them. For three days and three nights they taunted and tormented and beat the girl. They denied her access to the pail in the cell used as a toilet and the terrorized child became incontinent, which is when they mocked her and kicked her and spit into the thin broth served to all inmates. Warsaw's true whores had been given free reign with someone they could feel superior to.

At the end of three days Renata was released into the custody of another policeman. "Say hello to the Gestapo!" The prostitutes waved her off.

"I'm taking you to your people," the Polish policeman blandly informed the filthy, stinking and terrified child. At one of the Ghetto's several gated entrances the policeman stopped, unzipped his pants, and relieved himself against the Ghetto wall. The hunted animal became an alert animal. Renata spotted a hole in the wall. On their odyssey through the countryside Janka had updated Renata on current conditions in the outdoor prison penning in the Jews. While the cop's pants were still down Renata leapt through the hole dug by children on the other side, knowing an adult could not follow her there.

In the summer of 1942, the Ghetto was being culled of its old, its sick, its homeless, and its orphaned. Renata was hiding on a roof as she watched the director of the Ghetto's ever-expanding orphanage march through the streets, singing, with 200 of his charges. He was leading them to the cattle trains, which were waiting for them all. When they were removed from view Renata descended the roof and questioned her brother.

"If Dr. Korczak went with the children, how come we aren't going too?" In horror, Alek stared at his little sister. He said nothing. His answer came several days later.

"I've got you into a work detail that will be leaving the Ghetto. Once you're on the outside, you will be approached by a Polish policeman who is going to arrest you. Don't try to resist him, and don't be afraid. He's on our side."

Finally, Renata perceived the true nature of the transports. She followed her brother's instructions without protest, and was arrested without incident. The policeman winked at her, and led her to his home. Hovering in the background, like a guardian angel, was Janka.

While Renata resided in the sanctuary provided by the policeman and his family, Janka went to work arranging false identity documents, and another safe house. When neighbours grew suspicious, Renata was removed. As Janka kept watch and detected the questioning looks and the wagging of tongues Renata was removed, and moved again. Running out of available safe houses, Janka resorted to locking up Renata in her brother-in-law's rat-infested tool shed. His job as a bricklayer kept him away during the day. In the evenings Janka plied him with vodka and his wife went to bed with him so that he would be unable, or too indifferent, to inform on them. These were desperate measures, and couldn't be kept up for long. In the next apartment Renata was moved to she was so quickly spotted, denounced and arrested that even Janka was unable to save her. It was Ania who came to the rescue then.

The policeman who arrested her beat Renata and she broke, confessing the crime of her Jewish identity. As she languished in the prison cell, expecting to be taken to the Gestapo, a dark-haired woman with dark, slanted eyes and high, wide cheekbones, a brazen young woman with a manner of the streets, barged through the doors of the station and strode up to the policeman on duty. From behind bars, Renata gasped. It was her sister Ania.

"Let her out!" Ania barked at the policeman.

"Have you taken leave of your senses, woman?! Do want me to arrest you too?!"

"Let her go." Ania confronted the policeman like Moses confronting Pharaoh. "I used to work for the family. They were good to me. I promised her mother I'd take care of her." That last part was true. "Look," Ania began to negotiate, "if you hand her over to the Germans you'll get nothing. I'll pay you for her. How much do you want?"

The cop considered the offer. "Fifteen thousand *zlotys*."

Ania opened her purse. "I don't have that much on me. I'll give you what I've got and I'll bring the rest tomorrow, but you've got to give me the girl now." The corrupt cop accepted Ania's offer. He released Renata, and the two Jewish sisters, stone-faced, walked out of the police station, free.

Ania kept her word to the cop. The next day she returned to the station and paid the balance owing on Renata's life. Most likely, the money came from Janka.

A time came when the policeman would pay. Ultimately The Polish Underground executed him. Not for blackmailing captured Jews, but for collaborating with the Germans.

After this electrifyingly narrow escape, Janka kept Renata close. Natalia's housekeeper chose homelessness, rather than abandon Natalia's child. The nanny and her charge slept side by side on the platforms of train stations, pretending they were waiting for the train. On cold nights Janka and Renata snuck into cellars and attics and slept there, creeping out again before morning light. When the weather was clement they curled up in ditches, and huddled together in open fields. They stole potatoes and carrots to keep from starving, and they stole coal from stationary freight cars on the outskirts of town. Anticipating winter, in the autumn of 1942 coal became as valuable as gold. Janka and Renata took turns scrambling up the ladders attached to the sides of the roofless cars, tossing down heavy black lumps to each other. Then they would return to the city and sell their booty. Janka and Renata had to fight for the fuel with street toughs, who clambered up the freight cars for the same purpose.

Janka taught Renata the language of the streets. She insisted the Jewish girl learn to swear and curse like a hardened hoodlum. Renata was a quick study, but not quick enough. Janka goaded and provoked until, exasperated, Renata blasted, "Fuck off!"

"Bravo!" Janka applauded like a demented professor. "Now you've got it!"

Winter was coming, and Warsaw was unreasonably dangerous for Jews. They could not continue living in the streets. Janka sent out feelers to farmers she bartered with. By November, in a hamlet located between Radzymin and Wolomin, Janka and Renata had farmed themselves out as hired hands.

Janka and Renata slept in the barn. The farmer, his wife, his toddler, and his mother-in-law resided in the main house. The farmer had a city cousin. Henryk, a young man in his early twenties, had joined a cell of partisans hiding in the forest. He used his cousin's farm as a base, coming in to eat and to bring food to his gang. When Henryk was in residence he, too, slept in the barn. Henryk seemed a quiet young man.

During the first week of their employment, Janka trained Renata. Under Janka's tutelage Renata learned to feed the pigs, spread manure, and harvest potatoes. Henryk kept a watchful eye. When Renata made a mistake and hurt her hands, and when her palms became calloused from the unaccustomed work, she felt compelled to hide them. Their employer believed he had hired experienced hands.

After the first week on the farm, seeing that Renata could hold her own and believing her charge was safe,

Janka decided to return to Warsaw. "I want to get Alek out. If I can find a safe house for him, maybe I can convince him to escape. As soon as I can, Renusia, I will come back for you."

When Janka left, the assaults began. At night, in the barn, Henryk crossed over from his pile of hay and grabbed Renata. "Rebecca!" He hit her.

"What?! My name is Krystyna!" Krystyna was Renata's Catholic pseudonym; the name registered on her false identity documents.

"I know who and what you are, Rebecca," Henryk smirked. "If you want to live, you'll do what I want and what I say."

Renata was barely fourteen and sexually illiterate. She didn't understand what was happening until it happened. All the while she clung to the tin medallion around her neck and prayed vociferously to the Virgin Mary. Renata cried and Henryk laughed.

For the next five weeks Renata laboured in the fields by day, and nightly returned to the barn and the relentless rapes. Malnutrition suppressed her menses, so Renata was spared pregnancy. She was spared nothing else.

On Sunday morning Renata attended the local church with the farmer and his family. Henryk was not in attendance. One Sunday, Renata recognized a girl in a neighbouring pew. Before the war, they went to school together. Renata's former classmate smiled at her. The next morning, on the farm, a forester from the adjacent town came to arrest Renata.

"You've got a Jew on your premises," the policeman informed the farmer.

"What?! That's impossible. Krystyna can't be Jewish! She prays with us in church! If that girl is Jewish I'll run her through with my pitchfork! I'll kill her myself!"

The hamlet was so small and the adjacent towns so ill-equipped, that a co-operative group of farmers and foresters with horses and buggies worked with the police when transportation was required. It would be inefficient to bring in a sole Jew, so a forester was sent to pick up Renata after picking up three partisans who had been arrested and were being brought into the police station for questioning.

It was December. Snow blanketed the farm and covered the fields. It wasn't late, but it was already dark. Renata was ordered onto the front seat of the buggy, next to the forester. Three strapping young men, clearly non-Jews, sat sullenly in the back. Henryk decided to come along for the ride. The arrested men were his comrades. What they didn't say, they signalled with their eyes.

A full moon hung in the frigid air, like a lamp. The snow was high and the forest was still, except for the clip clop of the horses' hooves. The young men, seated behind the forester, began to negotiate, offering Renata's sexual services in exchange for their freedom. Becoming nervous and growing tense, the forester snapped at his passengers to shut up. Renata sensed sudden movement behind her back. There was a skirmish. One of the men had leapt upon the forester. The forester had no gun, but he had a knife. Instinctively he lashed out, and cut Renata's throat.

"Scram!" Henryk screamed at Renata, who seemed stunned into paralysis. "Beat it!" The partisan shrieked, as he and his buddies laid in, murderously, upon the trapped forester. "Run!" Henryk howled at the girl, and at the baleful moon. Renata's rapist was saving her life.

Henryk's wails shocked Renata into action. She ran through the woods, in the opposite direction to where the forester had been heading, in snow that was sometimes waist-high, her path lighted by a benevolent moon. Red drops splattered onto the plush white carpet of snow. Renata realized that she was bleeding. She wrapped her peasant's shawl tightly around her neck, as a tourniquet. The bare black trees bore silent witness to the wounded girl's dash for life and freedom. The full bright moon beamed on her until relieved of its post, at dawn.

Reaching the adjacent town and its train station in early morning, Renata edged her way onto the crowded commuter line, and arrived in Warsaw before the conductor had time to ask for her ticket. Pale, weakened, and in stinging pain, Renata dragged herself to the flat where her sister roomed with an old laundress. Ania had staged her own escape from the doomed Jewish ghetto. She gasped at the sight of her wounded sister. Ania hid Renata in her room and staunched the gash with vodka. The right side of Renata's neck was infected.

For the first time that Renata had seen, Ania broke down. She wept and answered Renata's unasked question. "Janka is dead." On that frosty December morning, while dressing the wound on Renata's neck, Ania invented a story. She told her little sister that Janka had been caught in a round-up in the countryside and shot there. It would be decades before Ania could bring herself to reveal the truth. Janka had been making one of her regular forays into the Ghetto; this time, to bring Alek food. She was hoping to convince him to allow her to help him escape. Diminutive Janka, with her loaded, unlidded basket, was negotiating with a sentry at one of the Ghetto gates. Usually Janka knew who could be bribed and whom it was best to avoid. Perhaps this sentry was a new recruit. Perhaps it was simply that Janka's luck ran out that day.

Ania was an eyewitness. In helpless horror she had been standing across the street, watching the pantomime of Janka's wild gesticulations. In 1942, German soldiers didn't engage in protracted debates with Polish women. The sentry ended the discussion by shooting the pest dead.

Janka's corpse lay in the street, in the snow, until a work squad pushing wheelbarrows for just this purpose tossed it into the barrow, and wheeled it away. No one claimed Janka's corpse. Except for those powerless to act, no one cared. If Janka had lived to Christmas Eve, she would've seen her thirty-fourth birthday.

The Polish foreign ministry's representative pinned a medal on my mother Renata's thumping chest, and placed into her trembling hands a plaque with her name on it, which read, in part, *Odznake Honorowa* "**BENE MERITO**" – "Honoured with the Order of Merit". As a microphone was placed to her lips and she attempted to speak, the old and sick woman reflected on her childhood nanny's two lost children, unknown even to each other who, even if they had survived, would never learn that a saintly smuggler and Christ-like thief, murdered at thirty-three, was none other than their mother.

AUTUMN 2013 AND WINTER 2014

HOW MY MUM CAME TO FORGIVE OMAR SHARIF

While the world was falling in love with him, my mother developed a distaste for Omar Sharif. I was mystified.
"Mum. What have you got against Omar Sharif?"
"He reminds me of Stefan!"
My next question was obvious. Mum's answer would've surprised anyone but me. "Stefan was my fiancé in the D.P. camp. He jilted me."
That's how I learnt of Mum's early post-war love. As displaced persons in a refugee camp under American occupation in Germany, Mum and Stefan fell in love and were engaged to be married until Stefan's father, an Orthodox Jew, emerged from a concentration camp and objected to the match. Both Mum's brother and sister married Christians. In the eyes of her prospective father-in-law, Mum was tainted by association.
Mum's fiancé wouldn't defy his father. Instead, he broke off the engagement. After decades and despite her stardusted marriage to my dad, the rejection still stung. Unwittingly, Omar Sharif became collateral damage.
In the 1990s, as her generation were becoming grandparents, my mother was visiting friends in their Montreal suburban home when she noticed a photograph of the couple posing with Omar Sharif. Mum's question was obvious.
"He's our *machatunim!* (in-law) Our daughter Debbie was married to his son, Tariq." When he grew up Sharif's son, the beautiful child who played his son in *Dr. Zhivago*, married a daughter of Holocaust survivors. The marriage didn't last, but it produced a son named Omar. Omar the Third. When the Egyptian-born film star came to visit his Jewish grandson he

stayed, not at The Ritz in downtown Montreal, but in the suburb of Chomedey, with his *machatunim*. The locals got used to seeing the international celebrity stroll their streets hand-in-hand with Debbie's little boy. When Omar the Third grew up he moved to Hollywood, becoming an actor as well as a gay rights activist.

Tariq would marry twice more, and produce two more sons. His second wife was Christian, and his third wife was Moslem. His father the film star bragged, "I have a Jewish grandson, a Christian grandson, and a Moslem grandson!"

And that's how my mum came to forgive Omar Sharif.

WINTER, 2022

THE END OF THE BEGINNING

Now this is not the end. It is not even the beginning of the end. But it is, perhaps, the end of the beginning.
Winston Churchill, November 10, 1942

It was midnight, and silent. Mannheim had not known a silent midnight in two years. Skulking in the bushes beyond the ruins of the *Rathaus*, Renata bided her time. The lights inside American Military Government headquarters were out; the moonless sky was black. Seizing the moment, Renata dashed across the grounds and raced along the flowerbed…

A jeep carrying two G.I.s sped through the debris of the devastated streets and screeched to a halt in front of an apartment that Chaplain Hasselkorn requisitioned for three Polish Jews who had passed on false papers. A young man and two young women, one, still in her teens, had been brought to him six weeks before by a Jewish G.I. The younger girl was caught in last-minute cross-fire while foraging for food. Crouching for cover in the rubble of a gutted home, she overheard a soldier trying to communicate with a German civilian in a guttural language, she knew, was not German. She waited for the G.I. to finish speaking. She skirted around the scraps of metal and loose bricks that littered the devastated streets, and ran after him.
"Jude!" She shouted.
The soldier bristled. "What?"
"Jude!" Renata pleaded, pointing at him. The soldier glowered. "Who the fuck are you?!"
"Jude! Ich bin Jude," Renata insisted, first, in desperation, and then with a resurfacing sense of hope.
"Oh Jesus!" Finally, light dawned. "You…?"

"*Ja! Jude! Jude! Ich bin Jude!*" Renata beamed, fervently shaking her head.

"Oh Christ!" The Jewish G.I. gasped in recognition.

"*Kom.*" Renata led the overwhelmed soldier to a cylinder along the riverbank in which two people huddled together. Slave labourers were denied access to German bomb shelters. Her friends Cesia and Shimon cowered inside. Renata spoke to them in Polish and gently coaxed them out.

The G.I. brought the three young people to the American Military Government headquarters, to Chaplain Hasselkorn. Chaplain Hasselkorn promptly ejected a German couple from a nearby apartment, and bequeathed the space to Cesia, Shimon, and Renata. Now they were standing at the apartment entrance.

"Hi!" The driver winked. "You guys ready?"

Cesia, Shimon, and Renata glanced at each other. Cesia wore a dress, and Shimon, a suit that Renata had "requisitioned" from the closet of the departing German couple. Renata wore a dyed white coat over her own dress, which she had converted from a khaki-coloured American army blanket. Designated the group's spokesman, Renata stepped up and responded, "Och Kay! Ve ready!"

"Well hop in!" The driver thumbed towards the back of the jeep. Renata turned to her companions, showing off her constantly expanding English vocabulary. "Okie Dokie. Let's go!"

Carefully, Shimon lifted Cesia into the jeep. She was carrying his child. Renata followed, carrying the bouquet she'd assembled from the contents of the flowerbed in front of the old *Rathaus.*

The G.I.s drove out of the city and onto the *Autobahn* to Heidelberg. Heidelberg had been unharmed on orders from General Eisenhower because he planned to install his headquarters there. Jewish G.I.s had stumbled upon a tiny synagogue in a narrow lane in Old Heidelberg that, curiously, was still standing. The jeep clattered over the cobblestones of the ancient town, and rode up to it. Inside, a buffet table was heaped with doughnuts, cold cuts, pretzels, jelly beans, Wrigley's chewing gum, O'Henry chocolate bars, wine, beer, ginger ale, cola and Florida oranges the size of sunsets. The G.I.s had obtained the food in much the same manner as Renata had obtained the bouquet.

Renata and her companions gaped. They had not seen such a feast in six years. "Take a load off. Relax!" While the soldiers added final touches to the table, Renata and her companions sat on the synagogue steps, and waited. An hour later, a canvas truck, flanked by a jeep, rumbled up the road. Chaplain Hasselkorn, accompanied by a pair of United Nations Relief and Rehabilitation Administration workers, leapt out and pulled the canvas aside. Wraith-like apparitions began to stir. The U.N.N.R.A. workers stretched out their arms, and skeletal hands latched onto them. Laboriously these spectres limped off the truck, their steps tentative, unsteady, like pencils attempting to walk. They'd been liberated from their striped camp uniforms, deloused, scraped clean, and then dressed in an assortment of ill-fitting and mismatched clothes. One by one, the figures filed off the back of the truck. There were thirty of them; all men. They were confronted by a shy young couple almost as emaciated as they were, and a grinning teenager cradling a long-stemmed bouquet in her arms. She was robust and rosy-cheeked, having already benefited by Seventh Army largesse. Instinctively, the silhouettes knew.

"*Amchu?*" they whispered, to the couple, and the girl.

"*Amchu,*" the three affirmed. One of us... There were still Jews in the world. There were still Jewish women. Their own women had been wrenched from them at the first selection. Was there a wife or a sister who had been spared? Were such miracles possible? How?

Rabbi Hasselkorn led the congregation into the synagogue. Shimon and Cesia were pronounced man and wife.

After the ceremony, the congregation gathered around the buffet table. The bridal couple, the maid of honour, and the guests, in a daze, exchanged tales of survival. Tears, dammed for years, flowed like champagne. The men were Polish Jews from a town called Radom. They had been deported together and had survived, together. Five weeks earlier they had been liberated at Vaihingen by the French. They had been placed in a village near Neuenberg, and were beginning to recover. However, the French commander in charge of the village had received orders to transfer them to a Polish D.P. camp, and he had been concerned about the treatment Jewish survivors were likely to receive there. He had approached Chaplain Hasselkorn, who had approached a Jewish lieutenant from Chicago, who had succeeded in having the Radomer Jews transferred to the American zone because his superior looked away.

The Radomer Jews were currently housed in an ancient castle down the road. The lieutenant had evicted squatting Germans, Ukrainians, and Latvians, had the castle cleaned, and the Radomer Jews moved into *Schloss Langenzelle*. Now they were attending a wedding reception. Only those capable of digesting solids, and strong enough to stand, had been invited to the wedding. The flesh of oranges, peeled by trembling fingers, erupted like sunbursts. Doughnuts, sprinkled with real sugar, sparkled like jewels on reverently held paper plates. With their treasures, the men shuffled to the wooden benches in the centre of the room. One of their number, a young man called Kaddish, moved to the front, to where the *bimah* had once been. Without prompting, without accompaniment, he sang Kol Nidre. *"All personal vows we are likely to make, all personal oaths and pledges we are likely to take between this Yom Kippur and the next Yom Kippur, we publicly renounce. Let them all be relinquished and abandoned, null and void, neither firm nor established. Let our personal vows, pledges and oaths be considered neither vows nor pledges nor oaths."* As Kaddish's clear tenor filled the hall, the gathering grew hushed. Heads were bent in contemplation; shoulders were stooped in sorrow. Kaddish concluded the prayer. Palms plunged into eye sockets as if, by so doing, they could press out memory.

Slowly the congregation rose and moved outside, into the courtyard. The sky was silver. The stones glistened. It was drizzling. An U.N.R.R.A. worker pulled out a *Leica* camera. "OK, Gang. One for the album." The congregation arranged itself into three rows: Shimon and Cesia in the middle, with Rabbi Hasselkorn standing next to the bride. The front row was kneeling. Renata perched on a soldier's lap. Kaddish sat on the damp earth, next to her. Renata would meet him again, in Canada, at her own wedding. He would become her brother-in-law. The U.N.R.R.A. worker aimed the lens. "Come on everybody. SMILE."

The group gazed into the May mist. Beyond their vision lay a maze of roofs caught between the river and the hills. They stared out from this fairytale town, nestled within a gorge, untouched by horror, atrocity, nor even time. The mountains hung on the horizon, and a train chugged along the banks of the Neckar: *the trains... the trains...* The group stared into an open future and, bravely, smiled.

SPRING, 1991

OUTTAKE

In the rain, on the road between Mannheim and Heidelberg, the dashing French captain with the regional English accent bumps along in a side-car next to the driver, a red-headed, strong-minded member of the Women's Army Corps. On a motorcycle, a full-lipped, ruddy-cheeked, melancholy-eyed girl roars past them. There is a bumper sticker on the back of her bike which reads, in Polish, *Shake well before using.* A stray goose wanders into the middle of the road. Unnerved, the female lieutenant runs over it.

"Cut!" The tough and flinty Hawks ordered his drenched technicians. "Dames," he muttered, commanding cast and crew to redo the take.

On the road next to the film crew, the military police waggled their batons and leaned their backs into a crowd filled with real-life G.I.s, W.A.Cs and members of U.S. Army staff. Among them milled displaced persons who refused to return to their native lands and couldn't find countries prepared to take them in. Renata's motorcycle sputtered to a halt. She spotted a *landsman* from the Bensheim displaced persons' camp.

"What's going on?"
"Film stars! From Hollywood!" Twentieth-Century Fox cameras were staggered along the ruined, rainswept streets. "Cary Grant! And a new one!" (Ann Sheridan was unknown to those who hadn't seen films since before the war.) "*Ach!*" The adult D.P. dismissed the youngster. "You are too young to remember."

He was wrong. Renata remembered. She remembered when her mother, who had studied opera in Vienna, took her to Jeanette MacDonald's musicals. She recalled when her father, who was a lawyer, contacted a colleague serving as Metro-Goldwyn-Mayer's representative in Warsaw, and obtained for his little girl a membership to the Polish branch of the Shirley Temple Fan Club. Idling the motor of her bike, Renata recollected weekends in Sochaczew when she and her buddy Agnieszka snuck through a garden which led to the back entrance of the *kino* run by Agnieszka's dad. In the darkness of the makeshift cinema the awakening maidens pined for Robert Taylor and Tyrone Power. They thrilled to the shimmering Dietrich and the ethereal Garbo. In the final scene of *Krolowa Krystyna,* the blank canvas of Garbo's pale and chiseled visage so impressed the pre-teen that, later, she would adopt "Krystyna" as a war name. A Jewish girl would never be named Krystyna.

"Here they come!" The crowd surged towards the actors and jostled the crew. "Miss Sheridan! Miss Sheridan!" Homesick G.I.s waved pens and scraps of paper at their perky "Oomph Girl". W.A.C.s and army staff secretaries felt their knees dissolve into unset Jello as their celluloid heartthrob rode past. Except for Renata, none of the displaced persons asked for an autograph. Except for Renata, they were too timid to dare. Ann Sheridan good-naturedly braved the crowd and signed her name for anyone who approached, including a young solitary figure she spied sliding off the seat of a motorcycle. The language barrier between them rendered Renata mute, but the haunted look in her eyes told a horrific tale.

    Conversely, Cary Grant held back. He was miserable in Mannheim. The Heidelberg hotel which hosted him was inferior. He was deprived of what he considered edible meals. He had to eat off tin plates, like the rest of the cast and crew, and when the make-up man disappeared he was obliged to apply his own. He felt the German natives covertly hostile to Americans. The actor trembled with as-yet undiagnosed jaundice which would ultimately interrupt production on *I*

Was A Male War Bride. Throughout this ordeal, his co-star and his fiancée kept him going. On weekends, Grant and Betsy Drake flew to Switzerland, joining Joseph Cotten and Orson Welles. Cotten and Welles spent the weekdays in Vienna shooting a picture on black market racketeering. The actors commiserated over plates of *pate de foie gras.*

Returning to the seat of her motor bike, Renata watched the film stars acknowledge the crowd. Revving her motor, she vroomed off to the hospital in Bensheim. Renata loved having a motorcycle. Her dad had one. Like Cary Grant, she rode in a side-car beside her dad. She was his precious cargo. In the vengeful wake of V-E Day, on Renata's behalf Russian comrades "confiscated" a motorcycle from a cowed German. Besides, she had to get to work! Renata had purposeful work. When the Bensheim displaced persons' camp was established, Renata applied to the nursing course offered by the United Nations Relief and Rehabilitation Administration. She was trained by their medical staff and then sent for further instruction to Frankfurt am Main. She worked in the Jewish ward of the *krankenhaus* now, and in the outpatient clinic inside the camp which cared for survivors who refused to be treated by German doctors.

Fifteen months before, most of Renata's colleagues were within sight of Palestine's shores. Recruited by the *Bri'ha* and caught by the British, at gunpoint they were shoved off the ship which carried them, onto three floating prisons, sent back to sea, and anchored at *Port-du-Bouc.* Alert to the shift in world opinion, the French government refused to use violence against the Jewish D.P.s. In a vindictive decision, Britain's Foreign Ministry returned the ship to Hamburg. Within a year, all who sailed the *Exodus 1947* vanished from the British camps and resurfaced at the port of Haifa, where they stepped into a newly formed army. The traumatized survivors were given the chance to fight back for the first time in their lives.

Renata was relieved to have missed the boat. Her brother was still in Poland. After his escape from Warsaw's burning ghetto, he was hidden by a Catholic woman because she wanted him. He was forced to fuck for his life. A son was conceived. Unwilling to abandon the child, he decided to marry its mother and rebuilt his life in Poland.

In the immediate aftermath of the war, Renata returned to her homeland. After six weeks of incessant nightmares, with the help of the *Bri'ha* she trekked back to Germany's American-occupied zone and registered as a displaced person at the Bensheim camp. Renata's deepest wish was to bring her brother out of Poland. She feared that if she succeeded in reaching the Jewish State, she would never see him again. Meanwhile, she applied for immigration to the United States. England was accepting charwomen, but Renata didn't want to go to England. The British were even less popular with the Jews than the Jews were with the British.

Until 1948, Canada was run like a restricted club, accessible mainly to war criminals. The ethnically-dominated garment trade managed to slip in a handful of tailors, but it was not until the country changed its government that the gate to this most sought-after of sanctuaries began to creak open.

In the Bensheim displaced persons camp, word leaked that Australia was offering a one-year contract to nurses to work on an immigrant ship. Renata applied, imagining that, if accepted, she would jump ship, marry an Australian and acquire an Australian passport. At the same time, from a Jewish black market racketeer she purchased, or believe she purchased a nursing contract in Canada. She paid for the contract with the money she managed to save since being able to work for money, instead of as an enslaved labourer.

Concurrently Renata was waiting for word from Australian authorities, as well as a summons to Butzbach, for the physical examination required by the Canadians. She passed their I.Q. test and truthfully stated that she was not, nor ever had been a Communist. The physical examination was the last test she was required to pass. When the time came, a stand-in took Renata's place in front of an X-ray machine. The stateless teenager who replaced Renata had clean lungs. In wartime, a bout with tuberculosis left Renata's lungs scarred.

Renata's application for a contract to work on an Australian ship was accepted. The same week she received word that she had passed the Canadian physical. The young woman was confronted with a decision which would determine the course of what proved to be a long and admirable life.

From my frost-laced bedroom window, late at night I stare out at the snow-coated roofs of Ridgewood Avenue. I turn on my TV, snuggle under a quilt, and watch flickering forty-year-old images, eternally young, frozen in time... *In the rain, on the road between Mannheim and Heidelberg, the dashing French captain with a regional English accent bumps along in a sidecar next to his driver, a red-headed, strong-minded member of the Women's Army Corps...*

As I watch, I remember my mother telling me a story about the making of this movie, just before she came to Canada. Mum chose to come to Canada only to discover that she had been fleeced. The nursing contract was a fake. For a time, Mum was compelled to become a cleaning lady, after all.

I wish I had more keepsakes of the postwar period. All I've got is a faded photograph of a full-lipped, ruddy-cheeked, melancholy-eyed young woman in an U.N.R.R.A. nurse's uniform.

The film fades, and the TV screen dissolves into tones of snow. Outside my bedroom window the wind whistles, the snow on the rooftops drift and I drift with it, into a light and disturbed sleep.

BETWEEN WORLDS

A collection of essays by S. Nadja Zajdman

Grateful acknowledgement is made to the following written competitions, anthologies and journals in which previous versions of these stories previously appeared:

BETWEEN WORLDS: originally titled CAUGHT BETWEEN WORLDS, *CaféLit* June 13, 2024

AN UNRECORDED PERFORMANCE: *OutLook Magazine* (Vancouver) November/December, 2012, P.31

A PORTRAIT IN TIME: *CaféLit,* March 29, 2024

THE MAN IN THE RAINCOAT: *CaféLit,* New Year's Day, 2024

OPEN HEARTED: *CaféLit* Sample Saturday, December 10, 2024
Storyhouse, The Preservation Foundation, April, 2020

WHAT'S IN A NAME: *CaféLit*, February 27, 2023

DON'T ASK: January 25, 2022

NANA: *Brief*, a literary anthology published in New Zealand, June, 2010, P.17

"DADDY KAYE": *CaféLit*, March 28, 2023
The Best of CaféLit 13, Chapeltown Books,. May 2024

UPSETTING SANTA: *CaféLit*, December 2, 2023

TUESDAY'S CHILD: *CaféLit*, December 16, 2021
The Cynic Magazine, December 2008 (Won Special Mention in their Christmas story contest)

NOT MARY POPPINS: published under the title **REMEMBERING MISS JANE:** *Montreal Serai Magazine*, September, 2015
Also published in *Maple Tree Literary Supplement* (Carleton University, Ottawa, Canada) February 14, 2013

THE SHOW MUST GO ON: *CaféLit*, November 20, 2019
Magnetism I, Bridge House Publishing anthology, Winter 2020

SOMEONE TO WATCH OVER ME: *Boomer Women Speak*, February 2008
CaféLit, October 31, 2020
The Memory Keeper, Bridge House, January 2021

THE BEST PLAY HE NEVER SAW: Chicken Soup for the Soul's special anniversary anthology *The Spirit of Canada*, June 2017

AN ANGEL AT OUR TABLE: The Memory Keeper, Bridge House, January 2021
Bridge House's annual short story anthology *Mulling It Over*, November 15, 2020
Chicken Soup for the Soul's anthology *Family Matters*, January, 2011
The Cynic Magazine, August, 2007

UNTIL WE MEET AGAIN: *CaféLit*, April 1, 2020
Silver Sage Magazine: June 14, 2019

HEY MA, LOOK AT ME: *CaféLit,* July 25, 2021
The Best of CaféLit 11, Chapeltown Books, July 2022

MIKEY'S VISION: CaféLit, June 1, 2020

INSULT AND INJURY: *The Memory Keeper*, Bridge House, January, 2021
Under the title INJURY on *CaféLit*, November 18, 2019
Magnetism I, Bridge House, Winter, 2020

SETTING THE TEMPLATE: *CaféLit*, June 20, 2021
The Best of CaféLit 11, Chapeltown Books, July 2022

COMMUNIST HOT DOGS, IN PURSUIT OF PETULA, AND A KISS FROM MARLENE DIETRICH: *The West End Times*, May 26, 2007
Montreal Serai, June 2, 2007
The Cynic Magazine, August, 2007
Still Crazy Literary Magazine: January 2008
Horizon Magazine: May 2008

MY SECRET ADMIRER: *CaféLit*, June 9, 2020
Silver Sage Magazine, Summer, 2018
Gull Lake Magazine: Summer 2008
The Cynic Magazine, August 2007
The Lake Champlain Weekly: May 5, 2004

OUR P.E.T: Chicken Soup for the Soul's special anniversary anthology *The Spirit of Canada*: June, 2017

BLOOMING WHERE WE'RE PLANTED, AND A TASTE OF HONEY: *The Montreal Suburban*, August, 2019
On *CaféLit* in a truncated version titled BLOOMING WHERE WE'RE PLANTED, July 4, 2023

REMOVING SOCIAL MASKS: The singular anthology *Covid 19, An Extraordinary Time*, Chapeltown Books, February 7, 2021

THE WONDERFUL WORLD OF TRAVEL, A TALE OF THE PANDEMIC: *Dave's Travel Corner*, December 15, 2020
Under the title THE REFUND, The *Intrepid Times*, January 11, 2021

LET THE GOOD TIMES ROLL: *CaféLit*, July 31, 2023
The Best of CaféLit 13, Chapeltown Books, May 2024

THE SOUNDTRACK OF OUR LIVES: *CaféLit*, January 22, 2022

ERIC'S SECRET: The anthology *You Should Never Kiss a Frog*, MacKenzie Publishing, July 1, 2023

INTENSIVE CARE: Storyhouse, The Preservation Foundation, April, 2020

FINDING MY FEET: *Silver Sage Magazine*, Winter. 2018
CaféLit, November 21, 2019
The Woods Reader: Autumn, 2020
Magnetism I, Bridge House, Winter 2020

MOUNTAIN GUIDE: Chicken Soup for the Soul's anthology *Age is Just a Number*, November 3, 2020
Under the title AMAZING GRACE in July, 2018, in *Quebec Writers Federation Writers*
CaféLit, November 11, 2022
The Best of CaféLit 12, Chapeltown Books, July 2023

EUREKA SPRINGS REVISITED: *Dave's Travel Corner*, April 22, 2013

GOING HOLLYWOOD: *Maple Tree Literary Supplement*, Issue 5, 2009

BENE MERITO: *Storyhouse*, The Preservation Foundation, March, 2020

HOW MY MUM CAME TO FORGIVE OMAR SHARIF: *CaféLit*, January 17, 2022
The Best of CaféLit 12, Chapeltown Books, July 2023

THE END OF THE BEGINNING: *CaféLit*, June 1, 2023
Good News…? Bridge House, December 2024
The Best of CaféLit 13, Chapeltown Books, May 2024
Under the title A WEDDING IN HEIDELBERG in *The Saturday Evening Post*, February 20, 2015

OUTTAKE: *Bent Branches*

LIKE TO READ MORE WORK LIKE THIS?

Then sign up to our mailing list and download our free collection of short stories, *Magnetism*. Sign up now to receive this free e-book and also to find out about all of our new publications and offers.

Sign up here:
   http://eepurl.com/gbpdVz

PLEASE LEAVE A REVIEW

Reviews are so important to writers. Please take the time to review this book. A couple of lines is fine.

Reviews help the book to become more visible to buyers. Retailers will promote books with multiple reviews.

This in turn helps us to sell more books… And then we can afford to publish more books like this one.

Leaving a review is very easy.

Go to https://amzn.to/3B5AftE, scroll down the left-hand side of the Amazon page and click on the "Write a customer review" button.

OTHER PUBLICATIONS BY BRIDGE HOUSE

The Memory Keeper

by S. Nadja Zajdman

In these eighteen linked stories, the reader accompanies our heroine Noela ("born on Santa Clause's Day!") as she develops from an insecure Daddy's Girl into a woman willing and able to stand on her own. Go on this journey with her as she meets challenge after challenge and as her relationships with all around her change.

The Memory Keeper is a collection of tales about a life well learnt in S. Nadja Zajdman's distinctive story-teller voice.

"A really lovely collection –I'm going to read mine again."
(Amazon)

Order from Amazon:

Paperback: ISBN: 978-1-914199-18-9
eBook: 978-1-914199-19-6

I'm a Big Boy Now

by Eamon O'Leary

Life was simpler then.

Your passport to an Irish boyhood in a less frantic, more adventurous age, reliving a time of skinned knees and home-made go-karts, clean dirt, Saturday night baths, and the kind of sweets that'd nearly cost you your teeth. Back when it always seemed to snow at Christmas, the summers were long and golden, and the friendships were forever.

Eamon O'Leary gives us a glimpse of uncomplicated childhood in *I'm a Big Boy Now*.

"Life through the eyes of a 4-6 year old in the late 50's early 60's. A great read and very funny." (*Amazon*)

Order from Amazon:

Paperback: ISBN 978-1-914199-64-6
eBook: ISBN 978-1-914199-65-3

Tales of the Unelected

by Dan Corry

Visit the hidden Whitehall world of the unelected special advisers.

Encounter their hopes, dreams, rivalries and compromises as they face the challenge of doing the right thing in a role full of tensions. See how they struggle with the civil service, accusations of being the source of leaking, politicians who need to up their game, negotiating with No 10, finding time with the PM, and worrying about physical attacks on their Secretary of State. All this as they try to keep some semblance of family life intact.

Dan Corry entertains and informs us well in *Tales of the Unelected.*

Order from Amazon:

Paperback: ISBN: 978-1-914199-70-7
eBook: 978-1-914199-71-4

www.ingramcontent.com/pod-product-compliance
Lightning Source LLC
Chambersburg PA
CBHW061637040426
42446CB00010B/1467